VEGE
COOKING

FOR STARTERS

Blanche Agassy McCord

Crystal Clarity Publishers
Nevada City, California

Library of Congress Cataloging-in-Publication Data

McCord, Blanche Agassy, 1958-
Vegetarian cooking for starters : simple recipes and techniques for
health and vitality / Blanche Agassy McCord.
        p. cm.
Includes bibliographical references and index.
ISBN 1-56589-153-8
1. Vegetarian cookery. I. Title.
TX837 .M475 2002
641.5′636—dc21
2002003634

ISBN: 1-56589-153-8

Cover photo by Barbara Bingham
Cover design by CA Starner Schuppe
Book design by Sans Serif Inc.

Printed in Canada
1 3 5 7 9 10 8 6 4 2

Crystal

Clarity

Crystal Clarity Publishers
14618 Tyler-Foote Road
Nevada City, CA 95959

Phone: 800-424-1055 or 530-478-7600
Fax: 530-478-7610
E-mail: clarity@crystalclarity.com
Website: www.crystalclarity.com

*This book is dedicated to all who are seeking
to grow in higher consciousness and love for all living beings.*

Contents

Contents

Preface

I was first introduced to vegetarianism in 1976 by friends who were inspired by the practice of yoga and meditation, as taught in India. I was about eighteen years old and living in Israel, where I was born and raised.

I started to eliminate all meat, fowl and fish from my diet. Instead, I ate more bread, cheese and salads. After a short time, however, I started to feel weak, and soon realized that my diet was not nourishing me properly. Gradually I became aware of the wonderful abundance of grains, legumes, vegetables, fruits, nuts and seeds that contribute to a balanced vegetarian diet.

Over the last 25 years, I have experimented with many different approaches to vegetarianism, including a diet that includes dairy and eggs, macrobiotics, veganism, raw foods, and Ayurveda. Drawing on my experience with the effect of these various diets on my health and sense of well-being, I have developed my own style of vegetarian cooking. This approach emphasizes the consciousness-lifting qualities of natural foods, with attention to nutrition, good taste and appearance.

Now I wish to be of help to you in your early exploration of vegetarian cooking. I am delighted to share with you the abundance and creativity of a plant-based diet, a diet rich in all the nutrients you need for health and vitality.

Whether you want to become vegetarian or you are just curious,

Vegetarian Cooking for Starters is for you. By following this simple guide, you'll learn to prepare tasty, nourishing dishes and easily create balanced, satisfying meals.

My best wishes for your perfect health,

Blanche McCord

Acknowledgments

It is my joy to present *Vegetarian Cooking for Starters.*

For the past six years I have been teaching cooking classes at *The Expanding Light* retreat. Last year Sean Meshorer, director of *Crystal Clarity Publishers,* asked me if I would write a book for people who are just starting to cook vegetarian meals. I was honored and grateful for the opportunity to share with a broader audience all the information I have gathered through many years of cooking and teaching. Thank you Sean for your idea, support and guidance along the way.

Special thanks to: Cathy Parojinog for her great job in editing this book, for her kindness, wonderful spirit and clear mind—it was a delight to work with her; to Sandra Kaftan and Graziella Arnoldi for their recipe contributions; to my husband Rich McCord for his endless support and love, for his willingness to try new recipes, and washing the dishes afterwards; and to all those who tried and gave me feedback on the recipes included in this book.

My deepest gratitude to my guru, Paramhansa Yogananda, for his Divine wisdom and inner guidance. And to Swami Kriyananda (J. Donald Walters), my spiritual teacher, friend and guide, for his vision in creating Ananda—an intentional spiritual community where people can grow in God—, for his vision of *The Expanding Light* retreat—where people can come and learn the secrets of true happiness—, and for inspiring me and many, many others to reach for the very highest in life.

CHAPTER ONE

An Introduction to Vegetarianism

Why Become a Vegetarian?

Perhaps once considered a strange lifestyle in Western culture, vegetarianism is now quite common in our society. Though each person's decision to adopt a vegetarian diet is usually based on a combination of reasons uniquely his or hers, there are three primary concerns that vegetarians may have considered. These are improved health, ethical and environmental concerns, and spiritual convictions.

IMPROVED HEALTH

As awareness of the role of saturated fats and cholesterol in obesity, heart disease, and cancer has grown, many Americans have adopted a vegetarian diet as a type of preventive medicine. Others say that there is more to be concerned about than just fat and cholesterol, that, in fact, human beings are simply not designed to property digest and thrive on meat. This view is based on the observation that the teeth and digestive tract in the human body are more like those of non-meat eating animals than that of carnivores.

Some question the safety of meat as a food, at least in the way that it is currently produced and marketed. Aside from the recent real problems of animal plagues that can infect humans also (such as "Mad Cow" Disease), there is a growing concern over the widespread use of antibiotics and hormones in the production of meat, and how human health may be affected by ingestion of drug-saturated meat.

ETHICAL AND ENVIRONMENTAL CONCERNS

It has been stated that if all the land currently used for animal grazing were put into grain, legume, and vegetable production, there would be no hunger and starvation in the world, as there would be ample supply to feed every man, woman and child a nutritious diet. Other concerns include: the rapid destruction of particular environments, such as the rainforest, in order to support the beef industry; mistreatment of factory-farmed animals; over-fishing of rivers and oceans, and the destruction of other species in the process (for example, dolphins that get caught in tuna fishing nets).

SPIRITUAL CONVICTIONS

A number of spiritual teachings, including those of yoga, Hinduism, Jainism, and many Native American and other aboriginal peoples, believe that all living beings are expressions of God. Therefore, all animals are equally precious embodiments of Spirit, and should be respected as such. The practice of killing animals for food is thus abhorrent to adherents of these religions and to be avoided except as necessary to sustain life (for example, in environments where there are few plant foods available).

What Do Vegetarians Eat?

As the name suggests, vegetarians do eat vegetables. But that is certainly not all we eat! I recall one particularly disappointing experience with what seems to be a common American concept of a vegetarian meal.

In 1994, while I was visiting friends in Los Angeles, we planned to have lunch at a highly regarded restaurant in one of the major downtown hotels. We made our reservations, specifically requesting a vegetarian entrée. I was really looking forward to the experience, because the restaurant had a reputation for exceptionally delicious food. To my dismay, our lunch consisted of ordinary pasta with red sauce, and plain boiled vegetables. Bland and unappetizing, it was essentially a meal from which the meat had been removed, but nothing at all interesting had been added!

A vegetarian diet can actually provide us with much more variety in tastes and textures than the typical meat-based fare. While the average American home-cooked meal generally consists of a piece of meat (or fish, perhaps), a starch (such as potatoes, rice, pasta or bread), and a cooked vegetable and/or salad, a vegetarian repast may be composed of a number of dishes combining legumes, grains, vegetables, nuts, fruits and seasonings.

And, not all vegetarians eat alike. Because of varying concerns about the quality and means of obtaining non-flesh animal products, there are differences in diet within vegetarianism. The three main approaches are:

OVO-LACTO VEGETARIANISM, which includes the products of animals obtainable without slaughter, such as milk products, eggs, and honey.

LACTO-VEGETARIANISM, which includes dairy products and honey but avoids eggs (as the embryos of potentially living beings).

VEGANISM, which avoids all products of animal origin, including honey and other bee products (usually based on a desire to avoid consumption of any food that involves the exploitation of animals).

In general, a balanced vegetarian diet is based on natural foods, including whole grains, legumes, vegetables, fruits, nuts, and seeds.

The Ideal Diet

Even fresh, natural foods have varying influences on our consciousness, which affects our health and happiness. The teachings of yoga recommend following a diet that promotes harmony rather than stimulation—one that keeps the nervous system calm and peaceful, and fills the body with energy, vitality and strength. According to these beliefs, all creation—and therefore our food—is composed of three subtle qualities, those that are elevating, activating or darkening. When we eat, or surround ourselves with, one of these qualities, our consciousness is drawn in that direction. By our awareness of these tendencies, and by choosing carefully how we feed our bodies, we can influence and shape our minds and lives. Here are some guidelines:

ELEVATING

Natural, calming and cleansing foods are elevating, as are foods that increase life, vitality, strength, health and joy. They draw us toward goodness, truth, purity and spirituality, and foster within us such qualities as expansiveness, intelligence, creativity, love, sympathy, calmness, patience, and devotion.

Elevating foods include raw fruits and vegetables, fresh raw milk and cream, butter and ghee, nuts and seeds, and dried fruit, as well as pure water, clean air, and sunlight.

ACTIVATING

Cooked, spicy and stimulating foods are activating, as are foods that are excessively hot, bitter, sour, or salty. They give us physical energy, and support such "movement-oriented" qualities as curiosity, initiative, creativity, liveliness, ambition, restlessness, impulsiveness, over-seriousness, and aggression.

Naturally activating foods include whole grains, lightly cooked vegetables and fruits, onions, garlic, eggs, cheeses, fats and oils, salt, refined sugar, soft drinks and coffee. Lamb, poultry and fish are also activating.

DARKENING

Overcooked, spoiled or unwholesome foods are darkening. They lead us toward dullness, laziness, inertia, negativity, anger, covetousness, deceit, lust, and body consciousness.

Darkening foods include moldy cheeses, deep-fried food, very hot spicy foods, overcooked food, and foods that are canned, frozen, over-processed, chemically preserved, or fermented. Alcoholic beverages, beef, pork and all dried meats are darkening.

One might think that to achieve perfect health and lift our consciousness, we would want to eat only elevating foods. But Paramhansa Yogananda, the great master of yoga, recommended a diet that includes foods with both elevating and activating vibrations. Why? For one thing, many people are unable to successfully digest (and therefore draw the life force from) raw foods. Also, most of us have active lives, with many duties and responsibilities that require physical energy and initiative. As Yogananda pointed out, we need to balance our need to fulfill these outer demands with the desire to seek a higher consciousness. Therefore, his recommended diet included whole grains (cooked), vegetables and fruits (raw and lightly cooked), low-fat yogurt, cottage cheese, milk, butter, nuts and seeds.

As you think about what kind of balance you'd like to achieve in your life and diet, remember that there are other factors at work also. Even though each food has its own innate vibrations, our consciousness and intention in cooking and eating that food can help us to infuse it with uplifting, more spiritually supportive vibrations.

The Role of Dairy Products and Eggs

Whole milk is rich in protein, calcium, and vitamins. Eggs are a wonderful source of high-quality protein, abundant B vitamins, and minerals.

They can both be part of a healthy vegetarian diet. However, mass-production farming methods, long-term storage, and long-range shipping requirements have greatly compromised the quality of most dairy products and eggs available in the markets today.

MILK

Many people, both vegetarians and non-vegetarians, have found that dairy products can contribute to health problems such as allergies, asthma, arthritis, and heart disease. Whole milk is high in fat and contains cholesterol, making it a poor choice for those who need or wish to limit their fat intake. In addition, some individuals lack the enzyme needed for digesting lactose, which is the natural sugar found in milk. The variety of reduced-fat and non-fat varieties of milk, cheeses, and yogurt now available has provided a partial solution, as has the advent of lactose-free milk products, but these are all highly-processed foods.

In the yogic tradition milk is believed to have uplifting, calming and healing properties—but only when the milk is produced by healthy home bred cows that are raised on natural feed, and not treated with hormones and antibiotics. In addition, the milk should be consumed shortly after milking the cow, and not be homogenized or refrigerated beforehand. Likewise, butter, yogurt and cheeses should be made with fresh milk, and not adulterated with artificial color and flavor. Fresh cheeses, such as cottage cheese or farmer style cheeses, are preferred. Finally, milk is considered to be a food in itself, and not as a beverage to be drunk along with a meal.

For the most part, the American dairy industry produces milk, butter, yogurt and cheeses that do not meet these standards. If you want to include dairy foods in your diet, look for a local, organic source.

EGGS

In recent years, eggs have been banned from the diets of many Americans because of their natural cholesterol content. Actually, the fat and cholesterol are contained entirely in the egg yolk, along with B vitamins and minerals; the egg white is almost pure protein.

Eggs are generally produced by hens kept in artificial indoor environments, and raised on feed laced with antibiotics and hormones to increase production. But there are sources of eggs produced by "range-fed" chickens that are not kept confined and are given natural feed without hormones or antibiotics. Some of these free-range chickens are fed only organically-grown grains, but not all, so it is important to read the egg carton carefully. Even so, these eggs may have lost some of their nutritional value through the time of transit and storage before retail sale.

ALTERNATIVES

For people who suffer from allergies to dairy products and eggs, or who simply do not want to eat them, there are many alternatives available in the market today. There are several commercially available brands of almond, rice and soymilk, and cheeses made from these same non-dairy sources. Egg substitutes, in both liquid and powder form, are also available, often in mainstream supermarkets. For recipes that call for eggs, you can also use ground flaxseed, silken tofu, or pureed fruit as substitutes.

It is also possible to create delicious and fully nutritious meals without use of dairy, eggs, or any substitute products, which is what I have done in my recipes.

What about Protein?

In the not too distant past, it was considered essential for good health to eat meat or fish for the "complete" protein that they provide. Attempting to compensate for this perceived lack in the vegetarian diet, early enthusiasts advocated food combining techniques that would allow the body to extract the elements of complete proteins from each plant-based meal. This was predicated on the understanding of the human body's ability to synthesize proteins from the building blocks of the eight essential amino acids present in foods. But because it was thought that all the necessary amino acids had to be present in the stomach at the same time, this was a cumbersome method, involving eating certain combinations of foods in exact proportions at each meal.

Fortunately, continuing scientific research has shown that, not only do most foods contain proteins, but also that the human body can synthesize proteins from amino acids ingested over a period of time. In other words, by eating an adequate, *balanced* plant-based diet that meets our energy needs, we will be providing our bodies with plenty of protein.

However, it is true that certain groups of people—the elderly, children, and pregnant women—have higher nutritional needs. For them, and for others with higher nutritional requirements or difficulties in assimilating nutrients from their food, it may be advisable to supplement a plant-based diet with small amounts of dairy products and eggs. If you have any question about the advisability of a vegetarian diet for yourself, be sure to consult with your physician.

A Word about Organic Foods

Organic foods are those grown or produced without the use of synthetic chemical fertilizers, herbicides and pesticides. In addition, true organic farming involves the use of organic matter (manure and compost) to enrich the soil, so that its nutrients are replenished constantly. Organically grown foods are usually more nutritious and more flavorful than commercially grown products. Not only is it better for our health to eat organic foods, but it helps to create a sustainable agricultural system.

To ensure that you are getting good quality organic foods, it helps to know the source—the farmer or company, and your grocer. Buying organic foods locally, with the seasons, will help reduce your cost.

CHAPTER TWO

The Plant Kingdom

The plant kingdom includes an abundance of foods, and makes up the vast majority of the human diet, whether vegetarian or not. The four main food groups within the plant kingdom are whole grains, legumes, vegetables and fruits. Nuts, seeds and the oils extracted from various fruits, nuts and seeds are also an important part of a vegetarian diet. But because of the density of nutrients in them they are considered best used in smaller quantities, as condiments or seasonings.

Grains

Grains have been the basis of the human diet around the globe for thousands of years. The word "meal" literally means "ground grain." Whole grains contain the majority of basic nutrients essential for life: water, complex carbohydrates, protein, fat, vitamins, minerals, and fiber. They contain no cholesterol and are naturally low in fat. Grains are filling, calming, and nurturing foods.

There are many grains that have been harvested from the wild or cultivated by man over the thousands of years of human existence. Each has its own character and history, as well as a unique flavor and nutritional value—based on its specific balance of nutrients, vitamins and minerals. For a well-rounded diet it is good to eat a variety of grains.

Whole grains are more nutritious and balancing than refined grains. A whole grain is one that retains the bran and germ that are a part of its composition. The bran provides fiber, and contains B vitamins, proteins, fats and minerals. The germ is rich in protein, polyunsaturated fatty acids, vitamins and minerals. Refined grains are stripped of the bran, and sometimes the germ.

The complex carbohydrates in grains provide the main source of energy for the body. These complex carbohydrates are composed of many sugars, or simple carbohydrates. During digestion, the larger carbohydrate molecules are broken down into these sugars which then provide the body with fuel. Since this digestive process happens slowly, grains can supply a consistent source of energy and help you maintain a steady blood sugar level.

The list below shows the incredible variety of grains available to us.

GRAINS

Amaranth

Barley

Buckwheat:
White raw groats
Roasted, cracked groats (kasha)

Corn:
Polenta
Cornmeal

Kamut

Millet

Oats:
Whole groats
Steel cut
Rolled

Quinoa

Rice:
Brown rice—long grain, medium grain, and short grain
Basmati rice—white and brown
Jasmine rice
Wild rice

Rye

Spelt

Teff

Wheat:
Bulgur
Couscous
Wheat berries

People who have sensitivities or allergies to gluten should avoid all forms of wheat, barley, kamut, oats, rye and spelt. Those with wheat allergies are generally able to tolerate kamut and spelt.

Legumes

Beans, peas and lentils are all members of the legume family. They are nutritious body builders—filling, grounding, and warming. Legumes are high in protein, and also contain carbohydrates, fiber, iron, calcium, zinc, B vitamins and other trace minerals. They contain no cholesterol and are low in fat. By including both legumes and grains in your diet, you will be getting the major nutrient groups your body needs for good health.

If you are just beginning to add beans to your diet, it is wise at first to eat them no more than once or twice a week. You may need to experiment to find out which beans are most appropriate for you, and how to prepare them. Some beans cook faster and are more easily digested than others. Generally, the smaller the bean, the faster it cooks and the easier it is to assimilate. Start with these first, as the intestines may need to adjust to digesting all legumes comfortably. The body will gradually produce the enzymes needed to break down the bean-sugars. Until then, you may experience some bloating caused by gases produced by incomplete digestion.

Chew beans slowly and thoroughly, and use the cooking methods recommended in the recipes in order to prevent gas. Besides soaking the beans, you can add herbs and spices that will make them more digestible. See Chapter 6 for more information.

COMMON LEGUMES

Aduki, or azuki, beans	Lima beans
Black beans	Navy, or white, beans
Garbanzo beans or chickpeas	Pinto beans
Great Northern beans	Split mung beans
Kidney beans	Split peas (green and yellow)
Lentils (red, green, and brown)	Soybeans

OTHER SOURCES OF PROTEIN (Soy & Wheat Products)

Seitan (wheat gluten)
Tempeh (a culture of cooked split soybeans)
Tofu (soybean curd)

Vegetables

The plant kingdom is rich with an abundance of vegetables—a wonderful source of vitamins, iron, calcium and fiber. They are light, moist and easy to digest when properly prepared. Besides providing nourishment, they help cleanse the body. Fresh vegetables are better to use than frozen or canned, since they contain more energy and nutrients.

Each season of the year provides us with different vegetables to help align our bodies to the rhythms of nature. For example, in the winter we have an abundance of root vegetables, such as winter squash, rutabaga, and turnips. These hardy vegetables help keep the body warm. Summer provides us with colorful, succulent vegetables, such as yellow squash, red peppers, and corn, which help cool the body. Many salad greens grow year round, providing a crisp, fresh source of fiber and enzymes. Shopping at your local farmers' market is the best way to get fresh, seasonal produce.

In the chart below, I have sorted vegetables into four groups by type. Perhaps there are some that you've never cooked or tasted before. Experiment with unfamiliar vegetables and combinations of colors, textures and flavors. Try some of the spicy greens, such as arugula and mizuna, to create more interesting salads.

Note that spinach, Swiss chard and beet greens contain oxalic acid, a

ROOT VEGETABLES	GROUND VEGETABLES	GREEN AND WHITE LEAFY VEGETABLES	SALAD GREENS
Beet	Asparagus	Beet greens	Arugula
Burdock	Artichoke	Bok-choy	Endive
Carrot	Bell pepper (green, red, yellow)	Cilantro	Escarole
Celery root	Broccoli	Collard greens	Lettuce:
Daikon (white radish)	Brussels sprout	Dandelion greens	Butter
Fennel	Cabbage (green and red/purple)	Dill	Green leaf
Ginger	Cauliflower	Green onion (scallion)	Red leaf
Jerusalem artichoke (sunchokes)	Celery	Kale	Romaine
Jicama	Corn	Leek	Mizuna
Onion	Eggplant	Mustard greens	Radicchio
Parsnip	Garlic	Parsley	Spinach
Potato	Green bean	Spinach	Watercress
Radish	Kohlrabi	Swiss chard	
Rutabaga	Mushroom (actually a fungus, but used as a vegetable)	Turnip greens	
Shallot	Okra		
Sweet potato	Pea (snow, sugar snap, regular)		
Turnip	Summer squash: Yellow crookneck Zucchini		
Yam	Tomato		
	Winter squash: Acorn Banana Butternut Delicata Pumpkin Spaghetti		

substance that binds with calcium and prevents its absorption in the body. They should be eaten only occasionally, or in smaller amounts, especially by people with a calcium deficiency.

Tomatoes, eggplant, potatoes, and peppers (red, green and chili) are all part of the nightshade family. Nightshades contain the alkaloid solanine, which seems to affect the calcium balance in the body and may cause headaches, arthritis and joint pain. Macrobiotics and Ayurvedic medicine recommend consuming the nightshade vegetables in moderation.

Fruits

Fruits are rich in fiber, vitamins and minerals and a source of natural sugar, which provides quick energy. They are low in protein and fat, and contain no cholesterol. Fruits and fruit juices should be consumed alone, as a snack between meals, since they are digested more quickly than other foods. Drink fruit juices in moderation because of the high sugar content.

It is best to eat fruits that are grown locally, with the season. They can be eaten fresh or dried, but if eaten dried make sure they are organically grown and unsulfured (sulfur is a preservative used in the drying process).

Seasonings and Condiments

The creative use of herbs and spices is an excellent way to enhance the flavors of food, especially when you are cutting back on fat. A little experimentation, practice and experience are all you need to get familiar with these natural additives.

When using condiments, be sure to avoid overdoing it, which can create a mish-mash of flavors. It is important that the herbs, spices and seasonings you choose complement and enhance the flavor of your foods, rather than detracting from or dominating them.

The following chart lists seasonings and condiments I use regularly.

SEASONINGS	OILS AND FATS	NUTS AND SEEDS
Sea salt	Sunflower oil	Sunflower seeds
Tamari	Safflower oil	Sesame seeds
Bragg Liquid Aminos	Sesame oil	Pumpkin seeds
Miso	Olive oil	Flaxseed
Vegetable broth powder	Flaxseed oil	Almond
Vegit	Butter	Walnut
Spike	Ghee	Cashew
Kelp powder		Pecan
Lemon		Pine nut
Garlic		Peanut
Ginger		Pistachio nut
Nutritional yeast		Nut butters
Dried sea weed (nori, kombu, hijiki)		
Dijon mustard		
Fresh herbs		
Dried herbs		

Natural thickeners
   Tahini
   Peanut butter
   Arrowroot powder
   Kuzu

SEASONINGS

Seasonings are generally used to bring out the flavor of food. Salt, lemon juice, tamari or Bragg, and vegetable broth are the most commonly used seasonings in vegetarian cooking. Seasonings also add nutrients to food, primarily minerals (as in the case of sea salt, seaweed, and vegetable broth) but may also contribute protein and vitamins (nutritional yeast, miso, tamari, and Bragg). Other seasonings are natural thickeners that can be used as substitutes for corn starch (an overly processed product).

HERBS AND SPICES

Adding flavor and aroma to food, herbs and spices also stimulate and aid digestion, prevent intestinal gas, and help with fat metabolism. Herbs can be categorized according to their ability to withstand heat. Fragile herbs should be added at the end of cooking. Robust herbs, and spices, can be simmered or cooked in foods for longer periods of time, infusing the dish with their aroma and flavor. If you are using fresh herbs in a cooked dish, add them toward the end of the cooking time so their delicate flavors are not lost.

Fresh herbs are becoming increasingly available in supermarkets and grocery stores. When substituting fresh herbs for dried herbs in a recipe, 1 tablespoon of the fresh herb equals 1 to 1½ teaspoons of the dried herb. The flavor of fresh herbs becomes more intense the more finely they are chopped.

When possible, buy dried herbs in leaf or whole seed form, rather than ground. Crumble the leaves and grind seeds immediately before using them.

FRAGILE HERBS	ROBUST HERBS
Basil	Bay leaf
Chives	Marjoram
Cilantro	Oregano
Dill	Rosemary
Mint	Sage
Parsley	Thyme
Tarragon	

OILS AND FATS

Oils are extracted from seeds, nuts and fruits (avocado), either by mechanical pressing (unrefined) or by chemical extraction (refined). Some mechanical pressing techniques involve the application or generation of heat, which will destroy nutrients in the oils. It is always best to buy organic, *cold-pressed,* unrefined oils because they are higher in vitamin content and are more aromatic and flavorful. They also do not contain any chemical residues.

To keep oils fresh, store them in the refrigerator, preferably in dark colored containers. If they are allowed to sit exposed to heat and light they quickly become rancid. Since olive oil solidifies when refrigerated, keep a small container out at room temperature for daily use. Otherwise, take the olive oil out of the refrigerator an hour before use so it can come to room temperature. Oils stored refrigerated in airtight containers will last for several months.

For cooking, sunflower, safflower and sesame oils are good choices. Though canola oil (also called rapeseed oil) is widely used also, some consider it toxic because it is highly refined. For that reason I do not use it.

Olive oil and flaxseed oil are good for salads and dressings. When buying olive oil, choose organic, extra-virgin, cold-pressed oil. Flaxseed oil is very volatile, and goes rancid quickly, so look for it in the refrigerated section of your grocery or natural food store. It should never be heated, should be kept stored in a dark container in the refrigerator, and consumed by the expiration date.

Butter is the solidified fat from milk. It is a saturated, animal fat and therefore generally best avoided by those concerned about heart disease, diabetes and other illnesses associated with high cholesterol and fats in the blood and body. However, for baking it is unsurpassed because of its flavor and its ability to withstand heat without becoming denatured.

Clarified butter, or ghee, is sometimes used as a butter substitute for cooking. It is a clear golden liquid made by gently heating unsalted butter and straining off the milk solids (the water evaporates). Ghee is said by yogis to aid digestion and it does not burn as easily as butter. It can also be stored at room temperature for many months without becoming rancid.

If you choose to use a margarine or another type of butter substitute, be sure to read the package carefully to avoid hydrogenated fats (also called trans-fatty acids) which are harmful to the health. Hydrogenation is the process by which oils are turned into solids or semi-solids, like margarine. The oil molecules are altered as a result, and react differently in the body.

Nuts and Seeds
Both nuts and seeds are a good source of protein, vitamins, minerals and healthy fats. Because of their high fat content they are best used in small amounts. Nuts and seeds used as condiments can be added to grain

dishes, vegetables, and salads. Dry-roasting nuts and seeds to lightly brown and crisp them, brings out their flavor.

To ensure their freshness, it is best to buy nuts and seeds in the shell. Shelling and chopping expose more of the nut or seed to the air, which leads to loss of nutrition and rancidity. Roasting and salting nuts also affects the nutrient content.

Nut and Seed Butters

Nut and seed butters are nuts or seeds ground into a paste. Americans are all familiar with peanut butter, which is practically a household staple. However, butters can be made out of almost any nut or seed. Those you will usually find in natural food stores are almond butter, cashew butter and sunflower seed butter, but there are other choices too. When choosing nut or seed butter, be sure to buy brands without added sugar or hydrogenated oils.

Sweeteners

Simple carbohydrates are referred to as sugars. They may be naturally occurring (as in fresh fruits, fruit juices, and dried fruits), distilled from other plant sources (such as sugar cane, beets, dates, maple sap, and malted grains), or produced by insects (honey). Naturally occurring sweeteners are whole foods. They contain minerals and other substances that help the body to process and absorb them without creating imbalances. Refined white and brown cane sugars are pure carbohydrate, lacking those balancing factors, and are best avoided. Over-consumption of refined sugars can produce a relative protein deficiency, create a strain on the adrenal glands, and weaken the body overall.

It is natural to like sweet tastes and enjoy them as part of a balanced diet. Some people feel a meal is not complete if it does not include dessert. But if you find yourself eating a lot of sweets, and craving more, it may be a symptom of a nutritional imbalance. Reevaluate your diet to be sure you are eating enough protein.

If you feel that your desire for sweets is merely a habit, try satisfying yourself with spiced herbal tea, whole grain bread, fresh or dried fruits, sweet vegetables such as carrots or yams, or dairy products such as yogurt. Keep healthy snacks at hand and avoid getting really hungry, since sugar cravings become exaggerated when you skip a meal or don't eat enough. Be conscious of the sugar content in foods, and be aware that even "natural" foods can be high in sugar.

SWEETENERS

Barley malt
Brown rice syrup
Date sugar
Honey

Maple syrup
Molasses (unsulfured)
Succanat
Stevia (also called Honey leaf)

Beverages

For optimum health, stimulating caffeine drinks such as soft drinks, coffee and black tea are not recommended. They give the body and mind a quick blast of energy, but if overused actually deplete the system. Alternative choices include herb tea, decaffeinated tea, and coffee substitutes made from roasted grains and seeds.

Grain beverages—several known brands are Inka, Cafix and Pero—can be found in natural food stores and some supermarkets. They are sold in powder form which dissolves in hot water to produce a rich coffee-like flavor that is completely free of caffeine. There are also now a huge variety of commercially available herb teas that are very flavorful and satisfying.

Milk should be considered a food, not a beverage, and is not recommended unless you have a fresh, organic source. For use on cereal, in hot drinks and for making smoothies, nut, seed, rice and soy beverages can be substituted for milk. You can make your own nut and seed milks, or buy them, and rice and soymilk, in the health food section of your grocery store.

Fresh and canned fruit juices are available in a variety of combinations, or you can juice and blend your own. If you buy fresh or canned juice, be sure to avoid those with added sugar. Fruit juices are naturally high in sugar, without the fiber to help balance the effect on the body, so they can cause quick sugar "highs" followed by an energy crash. If this is a problem for you, try diluting the fruit juice with water, and drink fruit juices only occasionally.

CHAPTER THREE

❖

Conscious Cooking and Healthy Living

The most important aspect of any food preparation is to remember that the quality of the energy you put into your cooking will be reflected in the food itself, and in how you feel after eating it.

Changing the way you cook and eat requires time, planning and patience. While we know that physical food supplies the body with energy, we must also remember that good thoughts are nourishing food for the mind. Therefore, a positive attitude is an important ingredient to add to the process of cooking. Here are some tips that might help and guide you toward more conscious cooking and healthy living.

Spiritualize Your Cooking

- View your kitchen as a sacred place, a sanctuary, a place of worship. Keep it clean and orderly.
- Create a little "kitchen altar" with a photo of your loved ones for whom you are cooking as well as photos of saints, your spiritual guide, or others who inspire you. You may also want to add a candle and flowers.
- Pray and meditate before you start, so you'll cook with a centered, positive attitude and a loving heart. Avoid preparing food while in emotional turmoil.
- Practice gratitude, appreciation and thankfulness as you cook; it will create a more loving and sacred space.
- Use cooking as a self-offering and service to yourself and others.
- Pay attention and do things carefully, with focus, clarity and joy.
- Actively bring God into your cooking. Practice *japa* (repetition of the name of God), *mantra,* chanting, or positive affirmation, to keep you calm, centered and uplifted.
- If you listen to music, be sure it is soft and calming.

Spiritualize Your Eating Environment

- Try to make your dining area pleasant and uplifting.
- Once the food is ready, relax for a few moments before eating.
- Then bless the food—not as a mere ritual, but with conscious appreciation and gratitude.

At The Expanding Light retreat center, we sing a beautiful food blessing composed by Swami Kriyananda: "Receive, Lord, in Thy light the food we eat for it is Thine. Infuse it with Thy love, Thy energy, Thy life divine."

- It is a good practice to eat in silence, so you can concentrate on the food without distractions. Being aware of how you eat will help you to move towards a more conscious and harmonious way of dining.
- Treat your meal with love and respect, chewing the food well; this will help you better assimilate its physical nutrients.
- Concentrate also on drawing its subtle qualities, so you can better ingest harmonious, elevating vibrations.

Spiritualize Your Relationship with Food

- Eat only when you are hungry. Learn to distinguish between true hunger, and trying to fill a void caused by emotional upset, stress, or boredom.
- Don't overeat. When you finish a meal you should feel comfortable, and as if you still have room in your stomach.
- Avoid eating late at night. Falling asleep shortly after eating causes food to lie in the stomach without being properly digested.
- When you eat too much, or too little, or too quickly, accept it with humor and understanding. Resolve to keep trying to improve, and move forward.
- Make sunshine, oxygen, and energy a part of your regular daily diet. Bathe your body in the sunshine for a short time, every day.

Go outside and breathe fresh air very slowly and deeply in a re-laxed way for 10–15 minutes.

- Be creative, patient with yourself, and enjoy the process of trans-forming your diet.
- Remember that food is not just a bunch of nutrients; it is a part of Spirit.
- A great master of yoga, Paramhansa Yogananda said: "Once you learn to eat right foods and think right thoughts your body and mind, purified by this energy, will take on the beauty of the Spirit." *1930, Super-advanced Course No. 1, Lesson 12*

CHAPTER FOUR

❖

Foods to Buy
and Tools You'll Need

A Vegetarian Pantry

Here are some basic guidelines for what staples you'll want to keep in stock, and how to store them. Having certain basic ingredients always on hand will make meal planning and preparation much easier and healthier.

When storing food in kitchen cabinets, make sure to put items in airtight containers, and in a cool, dry and dark place.

WHOLE GRAINS—Buy a variety including brown rice, millet, quinoa, barley, and amaranth. Make sure that the grains you buy are fresh—you can tell by smelling them. If they are old, they will smell a bit dusty or musty. Store grains in airtight containers, and either refrigerate, freeze or place in a cool dry place.

PASTA AND NOODLES—Pasta generally refers to Italian Durum or Semolina wheat-based spaghetti, noodles, macaroni, etc. Other Oriental style "pasta" includes soba, udon, and buckwheat noodles. All pasta and noodles can be stored in the kitchen cabinet.

BREAD—Whole grain breads, whole wheat pita bread, and tortillas. Keep in the refrigerator or freezer.

CRACKERS—Low-fat crackers and rice cakes can be kept in the kitchen cabinet.

BAKING GOODS—Unrefined flours, and baking powder, should be kept in airtight containers and refrigerated or put in the freezer.

LEGUMES (beans and peas)—Buy a variety, either dried or canned, and store them in a cool, dry place, but not in the refrigerator. If you buy canned beans, be sure they don't have sugar added to them.

SOY PRODUCTS—Most soy products are sold either fresh or in vacuum-packed cartons. Soymilk and silken style tofu sold in these cartons can be stored in a kitchen cabinet, as long as it is cool and dry. Use them before the expiration date.

Fresh soymilk, soy cheese, tempeh and tofu should be stored in the refrigerator. Be sure to check the expiration date on the package. If you are buying fresh tofu in bulk, place it in a plastic container, and add fresh water to cover the tofu. Seal the container tightly and store it in the refrigerator. Change the water every 1–2 days and it will keep for about a week. Always smell fresh tofu before using it. It should not have any odor. When starting to get bad, it will smell slightly sour and the water will be cloudy. If it is not too far gone, you can try washing it in fresh water and cutting off the outer edges. If it still smells, discard it.

NUTS AND SEEDS—Store in the refrigerator in tightly covered containers. Some nuts, like walnuts, pecans, and almonds, freeze well.

NUT BUTTERS—If purchased in sealed jars, may be kept in the cabinet before opening, and refrigerated after opening. If purchased freshly ground, be sure to refrigerate immediately.

DRIED FRUITS—Store in airtight containers in the refrigerator.

OILS—If purchased in sealed bottles, may be kept in the kitchen cabinet until opened, at which time it should be refrigerated. If you buy oil in bulk at a natural foods store, be sure that it has been refrigerated there, and keep it refrigerated at home.

NATURAL SWEETENERS—Store in kitchen cabinet.

DRIED SEAWEED—Store in kitchen cabinet.

SALTY CONDIMENTS—Tamari and Bragg can be stored in the cabinet before being opened. Refrigerate after opening. Miso should always be kept refrigerated.

DRIED HERBS AND SPICES—Buy these in small quantities and keep them in tightly closed jars away from heat, light and humidity. They lose their flavor with prolonged storage, so ground and powdered herbs and spices should be used within three to four months. Whole spices and seeds keep for up to a year.

Buy fresh herbs only as needed. You can wrap them in damp paper towels and place them in plastic bags in the refrigerator. For those herbs that come in larger bunches (parsley, cilantro, and basil), place them stems down in a small glass jar, like a flower bouquet. Fill the jar with fresh water, and then loosely cover the herbs with a plastic bag (leaving room for air to circulate).

Useful Kitchen Utensils

There are a number of basic kitchen tools that will make your cooking easier and more enjoyable. You may already have some of them, so review the list below, and see what you might need to add.

BASIC TOOLS

CUTTING BOARD—Wood or plastic. If using wood, keep it clean with water and a vegetable brush. Avoid soap as the board may absorb it, and be sure to dry the board completely. You can protect it from cracking by rubbing cooking oil into it occasionally. Some people prefer to have two cutting boards—one for onion, garlic and other strong tasting ingredients, and another one for milder foods and fruits.

KNIVES—There are three basic knives that you need: a light vegetable knife; a small good quality paring knife with a sharp, pointed blade; and a serrated bread knife with a long, stainless steel blade.

VEGETABLE BRUSH—For cleaning vegetables and your wooden cutting board.

COLANDER—For rinsing vegetables, and draining pasta and soaked or canned beans.

FINE WIRE MESH STRAINERS—For washing grains and beans.

VARIOUS SMALL UTENSILS—Large cooking spoon, slotted spoon, ladle, spatula, tongs, wire whisk, vegetable peeler, kitchen scissors

MEASURING CUPS—Most sets include the four basic sizes (¼ cup, ⅓ cup, ½ cup, and 1 cup). Stainless steel is preferable because aluminum can get dented and the shape and size distorted. Larger sizes are optional.

MEASURING SPOONS—A set includes the four basic sizes (¼ tsp., ½ tsp., 1 tsp., and 1 Tbsp.). Stainless steel is best. If available, get also ⅛ tsp. and ½ Tbsp.

MIXING BOWLS IN DIFFERENT SIZES—Plastic or metal are fine.

BLENDER—For blending soups, making salad dressings and sauces, grinding nuts and more. Works better than a food processor for creating a smooth and silky texture.

FOOD PROCESSOR—For chopping, slicing and grating foods. Use instead of a blender when you have a large quantity of food to blend in a single batch, or the food is of a thick consistency (which is difficult for a blender to process).

FLAME "TAMER" OR DIFFUSER—A flat metal disk with holes and a handle that is placed on a gas stove burner, underneath the pan. It helps spread heat evenly and keeps food from burning or sticking to the bottom of the pan.

TIMER

POT HOLDERS

COOKWARE

POTS, PANS AND SKILLETS—Invest in good quality cookware as it will last a lifetime and makes a difference in the quality of your cooking. Stainless steel, cast iron, Pyrex, ceramic or enameled cookware are the best to use. Aluminum is a good heat conductor, but it reacts with food, leaving traces of aluminum in it. There is some cookware on the market now that uses a combination of aluminum and stainless steel for better heat distribution, and the food does not come in contact with the aluminum.

To get you started you'll need: a 1-quart saucepan with lid, a 2-quart pot with lid, a 10″ skillet with a lid, and a collapsible steamer, or a steamer-pot.

PRESSURE COOKER—Not a necessity, but it can be a real time saver. See Chapter 6 for more information.

RICE COOKER—Again, not necessary, but very convenient. See Chapter 6 for more information.

Measures and Weights

Using measuring cups and spoons is an essential part of successful cooking. As you get more experienced in using them, you will be able to calculate and multiply without needing a chart. It is helpful and useful to know, for example, how many teaspoons in one tablespoon, or how many tablespoons in one cup.

Note: When measuring, all cup and spoon measures are level, unless otherwise stated (such as rounded or heaped).

1 pinch = less than ⅛ teaspoon (dry)
1 dash = 3 drops to ¼ teaspoon (liquid)
1 tablespoon = 3 teaspoons = ½ ounce
¼ cup = 4 tablespoons
⅓ cup = 5 tablespoons + 1 teaspoon
½ cup = 8 tablespoons
¾ cup = 12 tablespoons
1 cup = 16 tablespoons
1 cup = ½ pint = 8 fl. oz. (liquid ounces)
1 pint = 2 cups = ½ quart = 16 fl. oz. = 32 tablespoons
1 quart = 4 cups = 2 pints = ¼ gallon = 32 fl. oz.
1 gallon = 16 cups = 8 pints = 4 quarts = 128 fl. oz.
16 ounces (oz.) = 1 pound (abbreviated as lb. or #)

HERBS AND SPICE MEASURES:

1 tablespoon fresh herb = 1½ teaspoons crushed (dry) herb = 1 teaspoon powdered (dry) herb

BEANS:

15 oz. can of beans = 1½ cup beans

ABBREVIATIONS:

tablespoon = Tb. or Tbsp.
teaspoon = tsp.

CHAPTER FIVE

Guidelines for Successful Cooking

Delicious meals, served by a calm, happy cook are the mark of success in cooking. Knowing your ingredients and how to use them is the key to a positive outcome. Using proper kitchen equipment is also important. To achieve satisfactory results with the recipes in this book, here are some helpful guidelines. Before you know it you'll be a confident and accomplished vegetarian cook!

- Before you start cooking, make sure to read or at least go over the rest of the chapters, as they prepare and guide you for the actual cooking itself.
- After you have done that, choose a recipe you want to try. Read the whole recipe beforehand, so that you will have a clear idea of what ingredients and tools you need.

- Make a list of ingredients and get them ahead of time. The recipes in this book all use foods you should be able to find in your local natural food store.

- Give yourself time to cook. It is best not to try new recipes when you have limited time as they might take longer than you have anticipated.

- First follow the recipe as it is written. This will help you to understand what was intended. The next time you do it, you may make changes according to your taste.

- You can double or divide any recipe in half without adverse effects. The only change will be the length of cooking time.

- The number of people to be served by each recipe is given, but it also depends on who is eating, and what else is being served.

- Cooking time depends on many factors. It will vary according to the altitude that you live in, the kind of oven or stove you use, the cookware that you are using, the size you cut the vegetables, freshness of your ingredients, etc. The cooking time indicated is to give you an idea of how long it can take to cook that specific dish. Use your judgment as to whether the dish seems done rather than relying solely on the cooking time given.

- Preparation time shown for each recipe refers to preliminary tasks such as chopping, blending, stirring, etc. All preparation should be done with focused attention, without distractions, when all the food involved is out on the counter top.

- When baking, bring the oven to the required temperature before putting in the food, unless otherwise specified.

- Managing your time:

    When making more than one dish, start with the dish that requires the longest time to prepare and cook. While waiting for a dish to cook, steam, or marinate, use the time to prepare another dish or other parts of the same dish. Cook quick dishes last, so the whole meal is done at the same time.

- Most of the ingredients specified in this cookbook will be familiar to you. However, a few are less common. Therefore, follow the recipes, and gradually you will become familiar with the new ingredients.

- When using tofu, keep in mind that different brands have a different consistency. Some brands of "firm" tofu will be harder than other brands. When tofu is too firm, it will take longer to absorb the flavor of a marinade. Adjust accordingly and experiment until you find the firmness that you like.

- Use of oils: Some of the recipes call for sautéing ingredients in oil. You can reduce the amount of oil; you need just enough oil to keep food from sticking to the pan. You can also begin with a water sauté, then drizzle in a very small amount of oil when the sautéing is complete.

- All recipes were tested on a conventional stove, with propane as fuel, at an elevation of 2,600 feet. At sea level foods will cook and bake faster, and at higher elevations they will take longer.

- If a recipe calls for an ingredient that you don't have, experiment with using something that you do have on hand, as long as it is the same type of food. For example, substitute quinoa or millet for rice, or tahini sauce for peanut butter sauce. Try to substitute leafy vegetables for leafy vegetables or ground vegetables for ground vegetables. You might like the new version better than the original.

- If a recipe calls for an herb or spice that you don't care for, omit it and add something you like. Make sure to allow for changes in cooking times and liquid quantities according to the substituted ingredients.

- Keep experimenting—it will help you to learn what you can and can't do in cooking. The knowledge will help you to gain confidence in your own creativity, so you have fun and enjoy cooking. (I would suggest, however, that you not experiment with new recipes when you are inviting people for dinner. It is better to make dishes that you are familiar with and confident will turn out well.)

- Make sure not to take cooking too seriously, for there are no absolutes. Ingredients, utensils, stoves and ovens can vary. Learning to be flexible is the way to become a successful cook.

❖

Essential Cooking Techniques

The way in which we prepare foods has a direct effect on the nutritional value of the end product. Food preparation techniques also affect the way the food looks, tastes, and feels in the mouth.

For those who are new to the preparation of grains, beans and soy products, this chapter will provide detailed directions for cooking them. You'll see that there is more than one way to prepare any of these three primary foods in the vegetarian diet. It is important to vary cooking methods as each has a different effect on the food and provides variety and interest to your meals. There are also a number of pre-cooking preparation methods that you can use. You'll want to learn them all so you can alternate or combine them.

Methods for preparing and cooking grains

PRE-COOKING PREPARATION

Rinsing (essential)

It is important to thoroughly rinse grains to remove dust and dirt that clings to the grain from harvest and storage. Here are the steps to follow:

- Measure dry grain first (it is difficult to measure wet grain accurately).
- Place grain in a bowl, and add cold water to cover it.
- Swirl your hand in the water to loosen any dirt or dust.
- Pour off the top part of the water with any floating debris, then pour the rest through a strainer. For very small grains (such as quinoa, millet, teff, and amaranth) you will need a finer strainer so that the grain will not be able to pass through it.
- Repeat 3 times or until the rinse water is no longer cloudy.

Soaking (optional)

Soaking makes grain soft, dramatically reducing cooking time, and making it easier to digest. However, it will make the cooked grain sticky. Grains you may want to soak before cooking are brown rice, barley, kamut, and wild rice. Here's what to do:

- After rinsing it thoroughly, cover the grain with water in a large bowl.
- As a general rule, let the grain soak for up to 8 hours. The longer you soak the grain the softer it will be. It is usually simplest to soak breakfast grains over night and cook them the next morning; and dinner grains during the day. If you soak grain more than 12 hours it will probably start to ferment. If you don't want the resulting

sour flavor, soak it for a shorter time, or keep it cool while soaking, perhaps in the refrigerator.

- Cook the grain in the soaking water, adding additional fresh water as needed. However, if you are soaking grains for more than 8 hours, change the water part-way through and use only the last soaking water for cooking.

Dry roasting

Grains can be dry roasted before cooking by any of the methods described below. It will give the grain a fluffy, light texture with a rich, nutty flavor.

- Place rinsed grain in a single layer in a dry skillet.
- Over medium heat, dry roast for 2–10 minutes, stirring constantly, or shaking the skillet every 30 seconds.
- Roast grain until it is fragrant and lightly browned. Some whole grains will pop when done.

Sautéing

Sautéing is cooking food quickly in a small amount of oil, until it turns golden or light brown. When sautéing grain, each kernel gets coated with oil, which keeps the grains from sticking together when cooked in water.

- Heat the oil in a skillet on medium heat.
- Add the rinsed grain, and sauté on medium-high heat, stirring occasionally, for a few minutes.
- Vegetables, herbs, nuts and seeds may be added to the sautéing grains, adding flavor and texture.

COOKING METHODS

Cooking liquid

Grains are usually cooked with water, but vegetable broth or fruit juice may also be used. The addition of oil, vegetables, herbs and spices to the cooking liquid will give added flavor to the grain dish.

Adding salt

Adding salt to cooking grain does not make it salty, but brings out the sweetness of the grain, and makes it more digestible. If you are soaking the grain, the salt should be added just before cooking. For one cup of dry grain, ⅛–¼ teaspoon salt is sufficient.

Steeping

Steeping and boiling are two different cooking methods. In steeping, less water is used, the grain is cooked in a covered pan, and all of the water is absorbed during cooking. This is the method used most often for making grain dishes.

> **To steep light grains, such as white Basmati or Jasmine rice, quinoa, and rolled oats:**

- Bring water to a boil.
- Add rinsed grain (you don't need to rinse rolled oats) and salt, lower the heat and simmer, covered, until the water is absorbed. Do not stir during cooking. (See cooking chart on page 33, for approximate steeping times.)
- Once the grain has absorbed all the water, remove the pan from

the heat and let stand, covered, for 5–10 minutes. This allows the steam within the pot to finish the process of cooking.

- Fluff the grains with a fork.

To steep hardier grains, such as wheat berries, brown rice, barley, buckwheat, millet, steel cut oats and oat groats:

- Put rinsed grain, salt and water together in the pot.
- Bring to a boil, lower the heat and simmer, covered, until the water is absorbed. Do not stir during cooking. (See cooking chart on page 33, for approximate steeping times.)
- Once the grain has absorbed all the water, remove the pan from the heat and let stand, covered, for 5–10 minutes. This allows the steam within the pot to finish the process of cooking.
- Fluff the grains with a fork.

Boiling

Boiling is ideal for hard grains like barley, oat groats, wheat berries, and kamut and works well for any grain that will be used in a salad. This method is like cooking pasta. The basic recipes in this book use **only** the steeping method for cooking grains.

To boil grains:

- Use 6 cups of water for every cup of grain.
- Bring the water to a boil, add the rinsed grain, and salt, and boil uncovered until the grain is done.
- Drain and serve at once as a hot side dish, or let the grains cool if you're making a salad.

Baking

Baking creates a nutty, soft, fluffy grain. It's a great alternative to steeping when you don't have enough room on the stove. The amount of water used in baking grains is similar to that used in the steeping method.

To bake grains:

- Rinse grain and dry roast it (optional).
- Place the rinsed grain in a baking pan or oven proof casserole dish.
- Add water, salt and seasoning, as required.
- Cover with a lid or aluminum foil, and bake in a preheated 350° oven, for the time indicated.

Pressure-cooking

A pressure cooker has an airtight lid, creating pressurized steam inside the cooker, which cooks the food quickly. Pressure-cooking seals in the nutrients of foods, making them more digestible and flavorful. It reduces the cooking time substantially compared to any other method, and saves energy.

Learning to use a pressure cooker well involves becoming familiar with your cooker, following the safety rules and instructions on use, and learning to recognize when it gets to full pressure. Once you know how to use it properly, you'll be amazed at how often you find it useful.

Caution: Do not cook amaranth, teff or noodles in the pressure cooker, as the foam produced in the process might clog the valve of the cooker.

Using a rice cooker

An electric rice cooker can also be used to cook other grains and beans, steam vegetables, and even to make soups, main and side dishes. There are some models available now that include an inner pot and a steamer to allow you to cook grains and steam vegetables at the same time. Once the rice or other food is cooked, the rice cooker automatically switches to "warm" mode, eliminating the possibility of burning the dish, and keeping the food warm without changing its taste or texture. For this reason it's a great tool for the beginner.

A GUIDE TO COOKING GRAINS

The following table gives an approximate guide for amounts of water, cooking times and yields for some of the grains. Cooking times will vary depending on the water used, the altitude that you live in, and if the grains were soaked. All information is based on using one cup of dried grain. When increasing the amount of grain, the amount of water decreases proportionately, because water evaporation lessens with greater amounts of grain.

GRAIN (1 cup dried)	WATER	COOKING TIME	YIELD
Basmati rice (white rice)	2 cups	15 minutes	4 cups
Barley (soaked overnight)	3 cups	30 minutes	4 cups
Brown rice (short grain)	2½ cups	45 minutes	3 cups
Brown rice (soaked overnight)	3 cups	30 minutes	3½ cups
Buckwheat (white & kasha)	2¼ cups	15 minutes	3¼ cups
Kamut (soaked overnight)	3 cups	60 minutes	3 cups
Millet	3 cups	25 minutes	3½ cups
Quinoa	2 cups	15 minutes	4 cups
Wild rice (soaked overnight)	3 cups	35 minutes	4 cups

Remember that for those grains listed above that were pre-soaked (barley, brown rice, kamut and wild rice) cooking times will be longer if they are not pre-soaked.

Methods for Preparing and Cooking Legumes

PRE-COOKING PREPARATION

Sorting and rinsing

Dry legumes need to be inspected carefully to remove any stones or shriveled and discolored beans or peas. An easy way to do that is to spread a small amount of beans, one thin layer at a time, on a tray and sort through them.

After sorting through them carefully, place beans in a bowl, add water, swirl your hand in the water and rinse. Repeat a few times.

Soaking beans

Soaking beans is very helpful for ease of digestion, as it removes much of the indigestible sugar in beans. In the soaking process, the beans swell as they absorb the water, so they will cook more thoroughly and in less time. The length of soaking time depends on the size and age of the beans. When soaking beans, the soaking water is not used for cooking, but is discarded.

There are two methods for soaking beans:

SLOW SOAKING: Place beans and water to cover them (3 cups water to every cup of beans) in a bowl and soak them for 6–8 hours, or overnight. If you soak them any longer, keep them in the refrigerator to avoid fermentation.

QUICK SOAKING: In a pot, cover the beans with boiling water (3 cups of water to every cup of beans), or bring beans and water to a boil. Boil for

2 minutes, turn heat off, and let stand for 1–2 hours covered. Drain, add fresh water and cook.

Split mung beans and lentils do not require soaking before cooking.

COOKING METHODS

Boiling
- After soaking the beans, drain and rinse them.
- Place the drained beans in a pot with fresh water, about 3–4 cups water for each cup of dry beans.
- Bring to a boil and simmer until the beans are soft, approximately 1–2 hours. (See the chart on page 35.) The older the beans the longer it will take to cook them. In order for beans to be digestible, they need to be cooked until very soft. If they are at all crunchy or chewy, they are not done.
- Keep the lid slightly ajar, and check periodically to see if more water is needed. The beans will not cook completely unless they are covered with water at all times during cooking. If foam forms on the surface of the water, skim it off and discard it.

Pressure-cooking
- Using a pressure cooker to cook beans reduces the time it takes to cook them by about half. The beans will be ready in 20–30 minutes (cooking and waiting time) if you have soaked the beans ahead of time.
- Use 2–3 times as much water as beans in the pressure cooker.

- Note: Do not cook lentils or split peas in the pressure cooker because they can clog the pressure release valve.

Tips for cooking beans, to aid digestion and prevent gas:

Cooking beans with a strip of kombu (see below) or with certain herbs and spices, will aid digestion and add mild flavor to the beans. On the other hand, there are some seasonings that should not be added to beans while cooking, as they will toughen the skins of the uncooked beans and increase the length of cooking time.

Add while cooking:

KOMBU—A dark green sea vegetable sold in dried, wide strips. Used as a tenderizing agent when added to the beans from the start of cooking, it enhances the flavor and aids in the digestion of beans. Use a 3" strip of kombu per 1 cup of dry beans. After cooking, you can cut the kombu into small pieces and allow it to blend with rest of the ingredients according to the recipe, or discard it.

DRIED HERBS—Adding dried herbs, such as bay leaves, rosemary, cumin, coriander, or fennel, to cooking beans will aid digestion.

Do not add until after beans are cooked:

SALT, TAMARI, SWEETENERS, AND ACIDIC FLAVORINGS, INCLUDING VINEGAR, LEMON AND TOMATO.

All these ingredients should not be added to beans until they are cooked all the way through and are completely soft.

In general, one cup of dried beans yields about 2–3 cups cooked.

A GUIDE TO COOKING LEGUMES

The following table gives the approximate amount of water needed, cooking times and yields for some legumes. Cooking times will vary depending on the freshness of the beans (fresh beans cook more quickly), the water used, and the altitude that you live in. All information is based on using one cup of dried beans, soaked overnight (8 hours) in 3 cups of water. The yield is for drained cooked beans. Without soaking, the cooking time will be half again as long (for example, 1½ hours instead of 1 hour).

BEAN (1 cup dried)	WATER	COOKING TIME	YIELD
Aduki beans	4 cups	1 hour	3 cups
Black beans	4 cups	1 hour	3 cups
Black-eyed peas	3½ cups	1 hour	2½ cups
Garbanzo beans	3 cups	1 hour	2½ cups
Great Northern beans	4 cups	1 hour	3 cups
Green split peas	3½ cups	50 min	2½ cups
Lima beans	4 cups	45 min	3 cups
Navy beans	3 cups	1 hour	2½ cups
Pinto beans	4 cups	1 hour	3 cups
Soy beans	4 cups	1 hour	3 cups

Vegetable and Tofu Cutting Shapes

HOW TO USE A KNIFE

Hold the knife at the end of the handle with a firm grip, keeping the tip of the knife on the cutting board. Hold the vegetable on the cutting board with the curled back fingers of your other hand. This will protect your fingernails and finger tips.

Cut by pressing the back of the knife straight down, through the vegetable, toward the cutting board. Continue lifting and lowering the back of the knife in a rocking motion, keeping the tip of the knife on the board and using the thicker part of the knife blade to cut. Move the vegetable toward the knife with the other hand, being sure to keep your fingers curled and retreating toward the end of the vegetable away from the knife.

CUTTING SHAPES FOR VEGETABLES

Cutting vegetables into pieces reduces their cooking time—the smaller the pieces, the shorter the cooking time. Fresher vegetables cook faster than those that are older. Root vegetables take longer to cook than leafy vegetables. Using a variety of cutting sizes and shapes will help you create a dish in which all the vegetables are done at the same time. It also makes cooking more creative and increases the visual appeal of the meal.

When a recipe calls for an ingredient to be diced, it means that it is cut into small cubes. Minced (typically onion, garlic or fresh herbs) means that the ingredient is chopped into tiny pieces.

Follow the illustrations below for the cutting shapes used in the recipes in this book.

Chunks

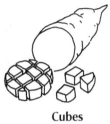

Cubes

Diagonals

Rounds

Half Rounds

Quarter Rounds

Crescents

Minced

Strips

CUTTING SHAPES FOR TOFU

Different recipes call for varying shapes, sizes and thickness of tofu pieces. Here are two examples based on beginning with a one pound block of tofu:

1. Cut into small cubes, size: ¾"x ¾" (36 pieces)
2. Cut into squares, size: 1½" x 1" (8 pieces)

Methods for Preparing and Cooking Tofu, Tempeh, and Seitan

Tofu and tempeh are high protein foods made from cooked soybeans. Seitan is also sometimes called "wheat-meat" as it is made of the gluten in flour, and is high in protein. All three of these plant proteins have a neutral taste, and tend to absorb the flavor of the foods and spices they are mixed with. Each of them should be cooked before being eaten, as they are difficult to digest in raw form.

There are several methods for seasoning and cooking tofu, tempeh and seitan, described below. Tempeh has more flavor and texture than tofu or seitan, and so may need less preparation. Experiment and see for yourself what you prefer.

Marinating

- This technique fuses flavors into the food, through soaking the foods in a flavorful liquid (a marinade) for a time period from 10 minutes up to overnight.

- Marinated tofu, tempeh, or seitan can be cooked by broiling, sautéing, baking, or adding it to casseroles, stews and soups.

Sautéing
- Heat a small amount of oil in a pan at medium heat.
- Place slices of tofu, tempeh or seitan in the oil and cook for 5–10 minutes, turning once. For more flavor, add herbs, spices, and seasonings, along with vegetables.

Steaming
- Usually used for tofu only, before marinating, in order to make it more digestible.
- Place sliced or cubed tofu in a steamer over boiling water and steam for 5–10 minutes.

Baking
- Place marinated sliced tofu, tempeh or seitan on a baking pan or tray.
- Bake at 350° for 10 minutes or longer according to recipe.

Methods for Preparing and Cooking Vegetables

PRE-COOKING PREPARATION
- Wash all fresh vegetables carefully to remove dirt, dust and grit.
- To preserve the vegetables' nutrients, peel and cut vegetables just before cooking them.
- The fresher the vegetables the less time you will need to cook them.

Boiling

- Add vegetables to boiling water in a saucepan, and cover the pan to allow steam to form.
- To minimize the loss of vitamins and flavor, use a small amount of water.

Steaming

- Place a steamer basket over 1–2 inches of water in a saucepan (the water level should be just below the bottom of the basket). Cover the pot and bring the water to a boil.
- Add vegetables (distributed evenly on the steamer basket), cover the pot again, reduce heat, and steam until the vegetables are tender.
- For vegetables with a longer steaming time (such as artichokes), check the water level periodically to be sure it doesn't all boil off.
- Steaming vegetables is generally more desirable than boiling them, as nutrients are leached out when the vegetables come in contact with hot water.

Sautéing

- Cook sliced or chopped vegetables in a little oil in a skillet on medium heat, stirring frequently.
- This method of cooking retains the flavor and nutrients of the vegetables.
- Many vegetables can be sautéed lightly before being cooked by another method.

Caramelizing
- This method of cooking is sometimes used for vegetables such as onion, celery or turnips to bring out their natural sweetness.
- To caramelize them, brown the vegetables in oil or ghee in a skillet over medium-high heat.

Stir-Frying
- Heat a little oil in a large pan or wok.
- Add sliced or chopped vegetables and toss them gently to lightly coat them with the oil. Cook over high heat while stirring continuously.
- Pour in little liquid (water or vegetable broth) and cover, allowing the steam formed to cook the vegetables until they are crisp-tender.
- Because stir-frying seals the outside of the vegetables and cooks them quickly it is an excellent way to conserve their flavor and nutrients.

Baking
- Place vegetables on a lightly oiled or foil-covered baking pan or cookie sheet.
- Sprinkle with seasonings, if desired.
- Bake at 350–400° for 10 minutes or longer, according to the recipe.
- Baking brings out the flavor and sweetness of vegetables in a distinct way.

Dry-Roasting Nuts and Seeds

Dry-roasting lightly browns and crisps nuts and seeds, and brings out their flavor.

- Place one layer of any kind of seed or nut in a dry skillet. Roast (without oil) over low to medium heat until fragrant, and light brown. They may begin to pop.
- Stir often or shake the skillet every 30 seconds for about 5–10 minutes, depending on the seeds or nuts.
- Remove from heat and let sit for a few minutes to complete the process of roasting.

For larger amounts of nuts or seeds, you can use the oven.
- Place one layer of seeds or nuts on an un-oiled baking tray.
- Place in a preheated oven at 350° for 10–15 minutes, depending on the nuts or seeds.
- Stir occasionally (every 1–2 minutes), roasting until fragrant, and lightly browned.

CHAPTER SEVEN

Some Basic Recipes

Grains

BREAKFAST CEREALS
Whole Oat Groats
Steal-Cut Oats
Rolled Oats
Basic Granola
Muesli
Coconut-Rice Cereal

SAVORY DISHES
Sesame Brown Rice
Herbed Rice and Amaranth
Tofu, Rice and Veggies in
      the Rice-Cooker
Wild Rice Salad
Quinoa-Carrot Pilaf
Buckwheat and Quinoa Salad
Golden Millet
Barley-Wheat Berry-Millet Medley
Summer Kamut Salad

Breakfast Cereals

OATS

There are three different forms of oats: whole groats, steel cut, and rolled. They all make a hearty hot cereal that can be seasoned with sweet or savory flavors and served for breakfast or dinner.

Oat groats are hulled, whole oat kernels with their bran and germ intact. Oat groats should be soaked overnight to shorten the cooking time. Steel cut oats are coarsely cut oat groats, and take about half as much time to cook if soaked. Rolled oats are quick to make and a soothing dish all year round.

◆

WHOLE OAT GROATS

Place in a pot, and soak overnight:
  1 cup oat groats, rinsed
  2½ cups fresh water

Soaking time: Overnight
Cooking time: 15–20 minutes
Serves: 3

The following morning, add:
  ⅛ teaspoon salt

Over medium-high heat, bring to a boil.

Reduce heat to low and simmer, with the lid ajar, for 15–20 minutes, until oats are soft and the water is absorbed. .

Turn heat off, and let sit covered for 5 minutes. Serve warm.

◆

STEEL-CUT OATS

In a pot on the stove, over a flame
diffuser, bring to a boil:
    1 cup steel cut oats, rinsed
    4 cups fresh water
    1/8 teaspoon salt

Cooking time: 25 minutes
Makes: 2½ cups
Serves: 3–4

Reduce heat to low and simmer, with the lid ajar, about 20 minutes, until all water is absorbed. the flame diffuser helps to prevent the oats from sticking to the bottom of the pan and burning.

Turn heat off, cover, and let sit for 10 minutes.

To pre-soak steel cut oats, in a pot, soak for 1 hour:
    1 cup steel cut oats, rinsed
    4 cups fresh water

Add:
    1/8 teaspoon of salt

Cook as above, but only for 10 minutes.

◆

ROLLED OATS

Bring to a boil:
    2 cups fresh water

Cooking time: 15–20 minutes
Serves: 2–3

Add:
    1 cup dry rolled oats
    1/8 teaspoon salt

Reduce heat to low and simmer, with the lid ajar, for about 5 minutes. Turn heat off, cover completely and let sit for 5–10 minutes before serving.

◆

BASIC GRANOLA

Here's a recipe to make your own granola at home. After mastering the basic technique, you can experiment by adding different ingredients to create your own variations.

Mix in a bowl:	**Baking time:** 20 minutes
⅓ cup maple syrup	**Makes:** 4 cups
⅓ cup sunflower oil	
1½ teaspoons vanilla extract	

Add, and stir until coated with the liquid:
     4 cups rolled oats

Spread mixture on 2 baking sheets (a thin layer of mixture on each tray). Bake at 350° for about 10 minutes. Remove from oven and stir and turn thoroughly. Return to oven for another 10 minutes, or until golden in color.

Take out of oven and immediately, while still hot, add and mix in:
     1 teaspoon cinnamon
     ¼ teaspoon nutmeg
     ¼ teaspoon allspice

Allow granola to cool completely on the baking tray, then store in an airtight container, at room temperature.

Variations:
Before baking you can add:
     ⅛–½ cup sunflower seeds or/and sesame seeds
     ½ cup nuts such as almonds or walnuts, whole or chopped

After baking:
     Immediately after taking the granola out of the oven, sprinkle over it and
          fold in:
          ¼–½ cup raisins, chopped dates, or other unsulfured dried fruit.

◆

MUESLI

Raw rolled oats soaked overnight with seeds and dried fruit makes a healthy nutritious summer breakfast.

In a bowl soak overnight, covered:
1 cup rolled oats
3 tablespoons shredded coconut
1½ tablespoons raisins or
chopped dates
1 tablespoon dried apricot, cut into small pieces
1 tablespoon sunflower seeds
1 tablespoon walnuts, chopped
1½ cups fresh water

Preparation time: 5 minutes
Soaking time: Overnight
Makes: 2 cups
Serves: 2 people

Next morning add:
¼ cup raw apple, grated

Mix well and add honey to taste.

Variations:
Add your favorite nuts such as: walnuts or almonds.
Add seeds such as: pumpkin or sesame.
Add your favorite unsulfured dried fruits.

◆

COCONUT-RICE CEREAL

Basmati and Jasmine rice are both aromatic long grain rices from the Far East. Basmati rice originates in India, and is sold as brown Basmati, with its bran and germ intact, or as a polished white grain. Both make an elegant accompaniment to curries and other savory dishes.

Jasmine rice is usually found as polished white rice, and less often as whole-grain brown. Known for its gentle, slightly flowery flavor and its sticky texture, it's a classic stir-fry accompaniment.

In this cereal, the white rice is enriched by the added protein of amaranth. It makes a hearty hot breakfast or a lovely dessert.

In a 2-quart saucepan, bring to a boil:
   3 cups fresh water

Stir in:
   ¾ cup white rice (Jasmine or Basmati), rinsed
   ⅛ teaspoon salt
   ⅓ cup amaranth, rinsed
   ¼ cup shredded coconut

Cooking time: 20–25 minutes
Makes: 3 cups
Serves: 3–4 people

Reduce heat to low and simmer, with the lid ajar, for 15–20 minutes until all water is absorbed. Turn the heat off, cover, and let sit for 10 minutes. Fluff with a fork.

Serve with honey and ghee to taste.

◆

Savory Dishes

SESAME BROWN RICE

Rice, in all its many varieties, is the most consumed food in the world. Brown rice is considered to be a perfect grain. It is the grain highest in B vitamins and is gluten free.

Short grain brown rice is heavy, moist and warming. When cooked, it is chewy and sticky—ideal for soups and puddings, or as a side dish with toasted sesame seeds, tamari and green onions. Because it is dense and energizing, it is good as a preventive care food during the cold months. However, some people have a difficult time digesting it. Experiment with different kinds of rice to see what works best for you. If Basmati, Jasmine or other white rice is better for you, you can improve its nutritional value by adding other grains, seeds, nuts, lentils or split mung beans to it, cooking them together.

When choosing rice, keep in mind that long grain rice cooks up dry and fluffy. Short grain rice is more tender and sticky. Quick brown rice has been briefly exposed to high heat. It retains its nutrients, but its texture isn't quite as good as that of longer-cooking rice. Combining different types of rice in one dish will add texture and interest.

In a heavy stainless steel pot bring to a boil:
    1 cup long grain brown rice, rinsed
    2½ cups fresh water
    ⅛ teaspoon salt

Preparation time: 5 minutes
Cooking time: 50 minutes
Makes: 3 cups cooked rice
Serves: 3–4 people

Reduce heat to low, cover and simmer for about 45 minutes or until all water is absorbed. Add ¼–½ cup fresh water during the steeping, if needed.

Remove from heat and let sit, covered, for about 10 minutes. Fluff with a fork.

While the rice is cooking, in a skillet dry roast:
    3 tablespoons sesame seeds

Add and sauté for 2–3 minutes:
    1 tablespoon sesame oil
    3 green onions, minced (about ⅔ cup)

Add:
 1–2 tablespoons tamari, or Bragg

Mix cooked rice with sesame-green onion mixture. Serve warm.

Variation:
 Instead of green onions, use 1 carrot, peeled and cubed.

◆

HERBED RICE AND AMARANTH

Amaranth is an ancient grain the size of poppy seeds. It is low in carbohydrates, gluten free and contains all the essential amino acids, making it a complete protein. Combining amaranth with rice will enhance the protein in the rice.

In a pot, sauté for 5 minutes:
 1 tablespoon sunflower oil
 1 teaspoon sesame oil
 1 cup cabbage, minced
 1 carrot, cut into quarter rounds
 Stems from 2 collard leaves (save leaves)
 $1/2$ teaspoon garlic powder
 $1/4$ teaspoon ginger powder
 1 teaspoon dried thyme
 $1/8$ teaspoon salt

Preparation time: 10 minutes
Cooking time: 15 minutes
Serves: 3–4

Add:
 $2^1/4$ cups fresh water

Bring to a boil, and add:
 $3/4$ cup white Basmati rice, rinsed
 $1/4$ cup amaranth, rinsed
 2 collard leaves, cut in strips (optional)

Reduce heat to low and simmer, covered with lid, until all water is absorbed and grains are cooked, about 15–20 minutes. Turn heat off and let sit, covered, for 5–10 minutes. Fluff with a fork. Before serving drizzle with tamari or Bragg.

If using a pressure cooker
Sauté the cabbage, carrot and collard stems as above in the pressure cooker.

Add the grains, salt, water and collard leaves.

Close the pressure cooker and bring to full steam, reduce heat to low and simmer for 4 minutes. Turn heat off and allow at least 10 minutes of natural cool down time (until valve goes down). Before serving drizzle with tamari or Bragg.

Variation:
You can roll cooked grains and vegetables in sheets of toasted nori. It will make 3 rolled sheets.

◆

TOFU, RICE AND VEGGIES IN THE RICE-COOKER

A convenient and quick way to make a whole meal in one pot by using a rice cooker. Following this example, you can experiment with your own one-pot meals.

Place in a large bowl:
    1 package (12 oz–1 lb.) firm tofu, cut
        into ¾ " cubes

To make the marinade, mix together in a small bowl:
    ¼ cup tamari or Bragg
    2 teaspoons dried basil
    ¼ cup sesame oil or olive oil
    ¼ cup fresh lemon juice

Preparation time: 15 minutes
Marinating time: 1 hour
(If you don't have time, skip this part.)
Cooking time: Approx. 20-30 minutes
Serves: 4

Pour marinade over tofu cubes, stir to make sure they are all coated, and let sit for 1 hour.

Mix in rice-cooker inner pot:
    1 cup white Basmati rice, rinsed
    tofu cubes and marinade

Add:
    2 stalks celery, chopped
    1 medium carrot, peeled and cut into quarter rounds
    1 cup frozen green peas, thawed
    2 cups fresh water (adjust according to your rice cooker)

Cover the rice-cooker with the lid and turn it on. The cooker will turn itself off when all the water has been absorbed, and will keep it warm. Fluff with a fork and serve.

Variation:
You can use different grains instead of rice, such as quinoa or millet. You can also vary the vegetables and herbs according to your taste.

Serving idea:
Serve with Lemon-Spinach Sauce, Garlic-Parsley Sauce, or Peanut Sauce.

◆

WILD RICE SALAD

Wild rice has a rich, robust flavor and is often used in stuffing, soups and salads. Actually an aquatic grass seed, rather than a grain, it is native to the North American continent. Wild rice is high in protein, B vitamins, and minerals. This dish adds color to a festive meal.

Place in a pot on the stove:
  1 cup wild rice, rinsed
  4 cups fresh water

Preparation time: 25 minutes
Cooking time: 1 hour
Serves: 6

Bring to a boil. Reduce heat to low and
simmer until tender, about 1 hour. Drain water, and set rice aside.

Meanwhile sauté in a pan for 10 minutes:
  2 tablespoons olive oil
  1 zucchini, cut into quarter rounds
  1 red bell pepper, minced (about 1 cup)

Set aside.

Mix in a bowl:
  $1/4$ cup olive oil
  2 tablespoons fresh lemon juice
  $1/4$ cup fresh chives, chopped
  $1/4$ cup fresh Italian parsley leaves, minced
  2 teaspoons dried oregano
  $1/8$ teaspoon dried red chili pepper
  1 teaspoon grated lemon peel

Place cooked wild rice in a large bowl, and add to it the sautéed vegetables and the dressing.

Season with:
  1 teaspoon salt, or to taste
  $1/4$ teaspoon black pepper, or to taste

Cooking tip:
Soaking the rice for 4–8 hours will reduce cooking time to 30 minutes.

◆

QUINOA-CARROT PILAF

Quinoa (pronounced "keen-wah") was the staple food of the ancient Incas. It is considered a complete protein, because it contains all eight amino acids, and it is also very high in unsaturated fats, calcium and vitamins. The tiny, bead-like kernels have a waxy protective coating called saponin, which will make quinoa taste bitter unless it is thoroughly rinsed under running water before cooking. Quinoa cooks very quickly. In the process, the germ, which is on the outside of the grain, unfolds, looking like a partial spiral.

Dry roasting quinoa gives it a nutty flavor. Baking dry-roasted grain produces a pilaf-type texture. This simple fat-free dish can be baked in a 9" glass pie pan to give it an elegant presentation.

Preheat oven to 350°

Dry roast in a skillet, and set aside:
¼ cup sunflower seeds

Preparation time: 10–15 minutes
Cooking time: 40–50 minutes
Serves: 3–4

Then dry roast in the same skillet until all
the moisture has evaporated and the grains have turned golden brown:
1 cup quinoa, rinsed well

In a 9" round or 9"×9" square baking pan, mix together:
roasted quinoa and sunflower seeds
½ teaspoon salt
1 teaspoon dried tarragon
1 cup carrot, peeled and cut into quarter rounds
2 cups fresh water

Cover with foil or a lid and place in the preheated oven, at 350 degrees.

Bake until all water is absorbed, about 30-40 minutes.

Remove from oven and mix in while dish is hot:
1–2 teaspoons ghee (optional)
¼–½ cup fresh parsley leaves, minced

Serve warm.

Variation: Use ½ cup quinoa and ½ cup Jasmine rice.

Serving idea: Serve with French Lentil Paté, steamed green beans and Tahini-Dill Dressing, or with Green Split Pea Soup, steamed collard greens and Peanut Sauce.

BUCKWHEAT-QUINOA SALAD

Buckwheat is not at all related to wheat, but is actually a seed that is a distant relative of rhubarb. It is commonly found in three forms: raw groats that are white, with hints of green, gray and tan; roasted, cracked groats—called kasha—that are a light reddish brown; and flour. Raw groats have a soft texture and a mild flavor, but roasting imparts to them a strong odor and taste. Buckwheat contains all eight amino acids and is high in vitamins and minerals.

Combining two high-protein grains, this salad is a deliciously light, healthy dish perfect for those who need to avoid wheat.

In a saucepan, bring to a boil:
    2 cups fresh water
    1/4 teaspoon salt

Preparation time: 10 minutes
Cooking time: 15–20 minutes
Serves: 4–5

Add:
    1/3 cup buckwheat, rinsed
    2/3 cup quinoa, rinsed

Bring to a boil again, reduce heat to low, and simmer with the lid ajar for about 15 minutes. Turn heat off, and let sit covered for 10 minutes. Fluff with a fork.

While grains are cooking sauté in a pan, for 5 minutes:
    1 cup onion, minced
    2 cloves garlic, peeled and minced

Add, and sauté for another 5 minutes:
    1/2 cup red bell pepper, diced
    1 1/2 teaspoons dried oregano

Turn heat off and add:
    1/4 cup minced fresh parsley leaves

After fluffing the grain, mix in the sautéed ingredients. Adjust seasoning by adding:
    1/4 teaspoon salt, or to taste.

Variation:
If you enjoy kasha, substitute it for white buckwheat groats.

◆

GOLDEN MILLET

The tiny golden seeds of millet are high in protein and vitamins. Millet is also gluten-free, easy to digest and has an alkaline effect on the body. Cooked millet has a texture that is easily molded or shaped, much like polenta. It is complemented by any kind of sauce.

Layering the grain over sautéed vegetables produces a light and fluffy dish.

In a large skillet or pot, sauté for 5 minutes: **Preparation time:** 10 minutes
    2 tablespoon sunflower oil **Cooking time:** 25 minutes
    1 cup leek, minced **Serves:** 4–5

Mix in and sauté for another 5 minutes:
    $1/2$ cup banana squash, peeled and cut into $1/2$" cubes
    $1/2$ cup carrot, peeled and cut into quarter rounds
    1 teaspoon dried thyme
    1 teaspoon dried oregano
    1 teaspoon dried sage
    $1/2$ teaspoon salt

Add:
    $1/4$ cup fresh water or vegetable broth

Then layer over vegetables:
    1 cup millet, rinsed

Cover and steam for 5 minutes, then add:
    $2^2/_3$ cups fresh water or vegetable broth

Bring to a boil, reduce heat to low and simmer, covered, for 15–20 minutes. Turn heat off, and let sit covered for 10 minutes. Fluff with a fork.

Cooking tip:
Dry roast the millet before cooking for a rich, nutty flavor.

Serving idea:
Goes well with Garlic-Parsley Sauce.

◆

BARLEY-WHEAT BERRY-MILLET MEDLEY

This combination of grains creates a highly nutritious dish. Barley, lower in fiber than most grains, is very easily digested. Wheat berries are the whole-wheat kernel, and are rich in protein and minerals. Because it is chewy after cooking, it is best eaten in small portions added to other grains.

Soak over night:
  1/2 cup barley, rinsed
  1/2 cup wheat berries, rinsed
  2 cups fresh water

Soaking time: Overnight
Preparation time: 5–10 minutes
Cooking time: 40 minutes
Serves: 6–8

Next day add to the soaked barley and wheat berries:
  4 cups fresh water (in addition to the soaking water)
  1/4 teaspoon salt

Bring to a boil, reduce heat to low and simmer, with the lid ajar, for 20 minutes.

Meanwhile, in a dry skillet toast over medium heat:
  1/2 cup millet, rinsed

Stir and roast until the grain darkens slightly, about 5 minutes.

Add millet to the pot after the barley and wheat berries have been cooking for 20 minutes, and continue simmering until all the water is absorbed, about 15 minutes. Turn heat off and let sit 10 minutes, covered. Fluff grains with a fork.

In a bowl mix together:
  1/4 cup olive oil
  2 tablespoons fresh lemon juice (or 1/4 cup for stronger lemony flavor)
  1/3 cup fresh parsley leaves, chopped
  1/3 cup fresh mint, chopped
  3 green onions, minced

Pour sauce over cooked grains. Add:
  1 teaspoon salt or to taste
  1/4 teaspoon black pepper or to taste

Serve warm or at room temperature.

Serving idea:
Delicious with Tahini-Dill Dressing and steamed or sautéed mixed vegetables such as beets, carrots, broccoli and sugar snap peas.

SUMMER KAMUT SALAD

Kamut (pronounced "kah-moot") is an un-hybridized form of wheat from the Mediterranean. About two to three times the size of modern wheat, kamut contains higher levels of protein and minerals. People with wheat sensitivity can enjoy this grain with no allergic reaction. Try this colorful, juicy salad in the summer.

Soak overnight:
    1 cup kamut, rinsed
    3 cups fresh water

Preparation time: 20 minutes
Cooking time: 1 hour
Marinating time: 20 minutes
Serves: 6

In the morning, place in a pot on the stove:
    soaked kamut and soaking water
    1/4 teaspoon salt

Bring to a boil, reduce heat to low, and simmer with the lid ajar until all water is absorbed and kamut is soft, about 1 hour. (Add more water if needed.) Set aside to cool.

Meanwhile, make the dressing by whisking together in a small bowl:
    1/4 cup olive oil
    2 tablespoons fresh lemon juice
    1 tablespoon Dijon mustard
    1/2 teaspoon salt
    1/8 teaspoon black pepper

In a large bowl, mix together:
    1 medium orange, peeled and segmented
    1 1/2 cups raw beet, peeled and grated
    1/2 cup green onion, minced (green and white parts)
    cooked kamut

Pour dressing over the salad and toss to coat. Let sit at room temperature for 20 minutes to allow the kamut to absorb the flavors.

Cooking tip:
Try substituting rice or quinoa for the kamut.

◆

Legumes

SOY FOODS

Baked Marinated Tofu

Crispy Herbed Tofu

Tempeh Croutons

LENTILS AND BEANS

French Lentil Paté

Mediterranean Navy Bean Spread

Black Eyed Pea Salad

Soybean Spinach Curry

Hummus

Pinto Beans Mexicana

Lima Beans with Lemon-Spinach Sauce

Lemon-Spinach Sauce

WHEAT GLUTEN

Seitan

BAKED MARINATED TOFU

Tofu is a soy bean curd, made from soybean milk, and a good source of calcium. There are many simple ways to add flavor and taste to plain tofu. You can use these marinades as basic ideas and gradually vary them according to your taste and creativity.

For each of the following recipes you'll need one package (12 oz or 1 lb.) of firm or extra firm tofu. One package will serve 3–4 people.

Preheat oven to 350°

Preparation time: 5–10 minutes
Marinating time: 1 hour
Baking time: 20 minutes

Salty flavor
Stir together in a bowl:
   2 tablespoons sesame oil
   2 tablespoons tamari or Bragg
   1 tablespoon fresh ginger root juice
   2 tablespoons fresh water

Sweet and salty flavor
Stir together in a bowl:
   ¼ cup tamari or Bragg
   1 tablespoon fresh lemon juice
   1 tablespoon maple syrup
   1 tablespoon sesame oil
   1 tablespoon fresh ginger root juice

Cut tofu into 12 pieces 1½" x 2". Add it to the marinade, turning the pieces over carefully to be sure they are all coated. Allow to sit for 1 hour.

Place tofu pieces on a baking sheet and bake at 350° for 10 minutes. Remove the tray from the oven and turn the tofu pieces over. Return the tofu to the oven and bake for another 10 minutes. Serve warm or at room temperature.

◆

CRISPY HERBED TOFU

This wonderfully textured tofu can be served as a snack, mixed with salad, or as a main dish for lunch or dinner.

Drain and wrap in a paper towel to absorb excess water:
Cooking time: 15 minutes
Serves: 2–3
    1 lb. firm tofu

Then cut tofu into 1 inch cubes.

Sauté in a pan, on medium-high heat for 5 minutes:
    2 tablespoons safflower oil
    tofu cubes
    1 teaspoon garlic powder, sprinkled on top

Sprinkle on tofu pieces and stir:
    1 teaspoon dried thyme (optional)
    1 ½ tablespoons nutritional yeast

Sauté, stirring frequently, until tofu pieces are golden and crisp on the outside, about 10–15 minutes.

Turn heat off and add:
    1 ½ tablespoons tamari or Bragg (or to taste)
    squeeze of fresh lemon juice (optional)

Serve warm or cold.

◆

Some Basic Recipes

TEMPEH CROUTONS

Tempeh (pronounced "tem-pay") is a cultured, fermented soybean product and has a much different texture than tofu. There are different kinds of tempeh, some made only with soybeans, some mixed with various grains, and some with added seasonings. It can be steamed, sautéed or baked.

These crunchy cubes of seasoned tempeh can be served with grains, vegetables, and sauces or sprinkled on salads.

Preheat oven to 350°

Cut into ½" cubes:
1 package (8 oz) of plain tempeh

Preparation time: 10 minutes
Marinating time: 2–4 hours
Baking time: 20 minutes
Serves: 3–4

Choose one of the sauces below to marinate the tempeh.

In a small bowl mix together:

Ginger-Garlic Marinade   or
¼ cup tamari or Bragg
⅓ cup fresh water
1 tablespoon sesame oil
1½ teaspooons fresh ginger
   root juice
2 cloves garlic, peeled and
   minced

Sesame-Tamari Marinade
⅓ cup fresh water
⅓ cup tamari or Bragg
2 tablespoons sesame oil
2 tablespoons sesame seeds

Place tempeh in 9" glass pie pan (or other ovenproof pan), and pour the marinade over it. Let sit for 30 minutes to 1 hour, then stir well to turn the tempeh cubes in the liquid so that all sides get covered. Allow to marinate for another 30 minutes to 1 hour.

Bake at 350° for 20 minutes, until all marinade is absorbed.

Variation:
If you're in a hurry, sauté tempeh cubes in safflower oil for about 10 minutes, turning them around until crisp and golden brown. Serve with your favorite sauce, such as: Italian Tomato Sauce, Orange-Ginger Sauce, or Tahini-Dill Dressing.

You can substitute tofu or seitan for tempeh.

FRENCH LENTIL PATÉ

French lentils are a dark green blue color and great in patés, soups, stews and salads. Lentils cook very quickly. An excellent way to enhance your protein intake, with a delicious paté that you can't have enough of. Goes with pita bread, crackers or tortillas.

Soak for 4–8 hours, or overnight:
    1 cup walnuts
    3 cups fresh water

Preparation time: 15 minutes
Soaking time: 4–8 hours, or overnight
Cooking time: 20 minutes
Makes: 3½ cups
Serves: 8

In a separate bowl, soak for 4–8 hours, or overnight:
    1 cup French green lentils
    3 cups fresh water

After soaking, drain both the walnuts and lentils.

Bring to a boil in a large pot:
    drained soaked lentils
    4 cups fresh water
    ¼ teaspoon dried red chili pepper

Reduce the heat and simmer, with the lid ajar, until lentils are soft, about 15–20 minutes. Drain water, but save 1 cup cooking water, and set aside.

In a pan, sauté until golden:
    2 tablespoons olive oil
    1 cup onion, minced
    2 cloves garlic, peeled and minced (optional)
    1 teaspoon dried oregano

Set aside.

In a food processor, blend:
    Soaked walnuts

Add and puree:
    cooked lentils
    sautéed onion and garlic
    ⅓ cup water from cooking lentils

Add and keep blending until smooth:
    1 teaspoon Dijon mustard
    ¹/₄ cup fresh lemon juice
    1 teaspoon salt
    ¹/₄ teaspoon black pepper

Add more water if the paté seems too dry.

Place paté in a bowl. Adjust seasoning, if needed. Drizzle olive oil on top of dish to prevent drying. Garnish with fresh minced cilantro or parsley leaves.

Cooking tips:
•Green or brown lentils work well in patés.
•Soaking the lentils reduces the cooking time by half.
•Soaking the walnuts softens them and makes them easier to blend. But you could dry roast them instead.

Serving idea:
Pita bread and a fresh salad round out a colorful lunch or dinner.

◆

MEDITERRANEAN NAVY BEAN SPREAD

Seasonings reminiscent of sunny afternoons at the beach in Greece or Italy enliven the delicate flavor of these small white beans. This spread is perfect with whole wheat bread, pita bread or your favorite crackers with salad.

Sort through, then soak overnight:
    1 cup navy beans
    3 cups fresh water

Preparation time: 15 minutes
Soaking time: Overnight
Cooking time: 1 hour
Serves: 4

Bring to a boil in a large pot:
    drained soaked beans
    3 cups fresh water
    3" strip of kombu (optional)

Reduce heat to low and simmer, with the lid ajar, until beans are very soft, about 1 hour. Strain and save cooking water.

Place in a food processor and blend until smooth:
    drained cooked beans (or 2½ cups canned navy beans, drained and rinsed)
    ¼ cup fresh water (or liquid from cooking beans, if any remains)
    2 tablespoons olive oil
    2 tablespoons fresh lemon juice
    1 clove garlic, peeled (optional)
    ½ teaspoon cumin powder
    1 pinch cayenne
    1 teaspoon salt (or to taste)
    ¼ teaspoon black pepper
    1 pinch turmeric powder (optional, to create yellowish color spread)

Garnish with paprika, black olives, and fresh minced cilantro or parsley leaves.

Cooking tip:
Add more cooking liquid (or water) for a creamier consistency.

Variation:
You can substitute garbanzo beans or soybeans for navy beans.

◆

BLACK EYED PEA SALAD

A colorful, tasty bean and vegetable dish.

Sort through and soak overnight:
   1 cup black eyed peas
   3 cups fresh water

Bring to a boil in a pot:
   drained and soaked peas
   3 cups fresh water
   3" strip of kombu (optional)

Preparation time: 25 minutes
Soaking time: Overnight
Cooking time: 1 hour
Marinating time: 30 minutes
Serves: 4

Reduce heat to low and simmer, with the lid ajar, until peas are soft, about 1 hour. Drain peas and set aside.

While peas are cooking, lightly steam in a pot, for 5 minutes:
   $1/2$ cup frozen corn, thawed
   1 medium carrot, peeled and finally diced
   2 stalks celery, diced
   $1/2$ cup red bell pepper, finely diced

Set aside.

In a large bowl combine:
   cooked black eyed peas (or $2 1/2$ cups canned black eyed peas,
       drained and rinsed)
   steamed vegetables

Then add to the bowl:
   1 tablespoon fresh lemon juice
   1 tablespoon olive oil
   $1/4$ cup packed whole fresh cilantro leaves
   $1/2$ teaspoon salt, or to taste
   $1/8$ teaspoon black pepper or to taste

Stir, and then let stand for at least 30 minutes at room temperature, before serving, to allow flavors to blend.

Variation:
You can substitute Great Northern beans, lima beans or navy beans for black eyed peas.

◆

81

SOYBEAN-SPINACH CURRY

Soybeans are an extremely versatile food—they can be eaten freshly steamed, dried and cooked, or made into tofu and other products. This tasty blend of curry and soybeans makes a special dish worthy of company.

Soak overnight:
    1 cup soybeans, rinsed
    3 cups fresh water

Preparation time: 5 minutes
Soaking time: Overnight
Cooking time: 1 hour and 15 minutes
Serves: 4

Bring to a boil in a large pot:
    drained soaked soybeans
    4 cups fresh water
    3" strip of kombu (optional)

Reduce heat to low and simmer, with the lid ajar, until beans are soft, about 1 hour.

After the soybeans are done, sauté in a large skillet on medium heat, until seeds start to pop:
    1 ½ tablespoons safflower oil
    ½ teaspoon mustard seeds

Add:
    2 tablespoons sesame seeds
    1 teaspoon curry powder

Mix in:
    drained cooked soybeans (or 2 ½ cups canned soybeans, drained and rinsed)
    1 teaspoon ground coriander
    ½ teaspoon turmeric powder
    1 teaspoon salt

Add:
    ½ cup fresh water
    6 cups, fresh spinach, chopped, arranged on top

Cover and simmer for 10 minutes. Serve hot.

Variation:
Instead of soybeans you can use garbanzo beans.

Serving idea:
Serve with Herbed Rice and Amaranth and steamed mixed greens.

HUMMUS

Garbanzo beans, also called chick peas, are a good source of protein and iron. This delicious Middle Eastern garbanzo spread is often used as a dip with fresh, raw vegetables or pita bread.

Sort through, then soak overnight:
$\quad$ ¾ cup garbanzo beans
$\quad$ 3 cups fresh water
$\quad$ 3″ strip of kombu (optional)

Preparation time: 20 minutes
Soaking time: Overnight
Cooking time: 1 hour
Serves: 5

Bring to a boil in a pot:
$\quad$ drained soaked beans
$\quad$ 3 cups fresh water

Reduce heat to low, with the lid ajar and simmer until beans are very soft, about 1 hour.

Blend in food processor until smooth:
$\quad$ 2 cups freshly cooked or canned garbanzo beans, drained and rinsed
$\quad$ ⅔ cup water or garbanzo bean cooking liquid
$\quad$ 3 tablespoons tahini (organic, roasted)
$\quad$ 2 cloves garlic, peeled (optional)
$\quad$ 1 teaspoon salt
$\quad$ 2 tablespoons olive oil
$\quad$ 2 tablespoons fresh lemon juice

Add and blend for an additional minute:
$\quad$ 2 tablespoons fresh parsley leaves
$\quad$ 1 pinch cayenne (optional)
$\quad$ 2 pinches paprika

Spoon hummus into a bowl and sprinkle olive oil on top to prevent drying. You can decorate with paprika, sprigs of parsley or mint leaves, and sliced or whole olives.

◆

PINTO BEANS MEXICANA

The earthy flavor of pinto beans makes them a favorite in Mexican dishes or as a substitute for kidney beans in chili. Here they are seasoned with both dried and fresh herbs and spices for a wonderful south of the border flavor.

Sort through and soak overnight:
1 cup pinto beans
3 cups fresh water

Preparation time: 5 minutes
Soaking time: Overnight
Cooking time: 1 hour
Serves: 4

Bring to a boil in a pot:
drained soaked beans (or 3 cups canned pinto beans, drained and rinsed, 2–15 oz. cans)
4 cups fresh water
1 bay leaf
1 teaspoon cumin powder
1 teaspoon ground coriander
1/2 teaspoon dried oregano
1/2 teaspoon dried basil
1/2 teaspoon garlic powder
1/4 teaspoon dried red chili pepper

Reduce heat to low and simmer, with the lid ajar, until beans are soft, for about 1 hour.

After cooking, drain off excess water and add:
1 tablespoon olive oil
1/4 cup fresh cilantro leaves, chopped
1/4–1/2 teaspoon salt or to taste

Serve warm or at room temperature.

If using a pressure cooker: Reduce bean cooking water to 2 cups. Close pressure cooker properly, bring to full steam, then reduce heat to low and simmer for 10 minutes. Turn heat off and allow at least 10 minutes of natural cool down time (until pressure indicator goes down). Continue with remainder of recipe above.

◆

LIMA BEANS WITH LEMON-SPINACH SAUCE

There are both large and small types of lima beans. The smaller of the two are sometimes called "butter" beans. The larger lima is the largest of the common beans.

The light summer green color of the garlicy sauce is perfect complement to these cooked lima beans.

Preparation time: 10 minutes
Soaking time: Overnight
Cooking time: 45 minutes
Serves: 3–4

Sort through and soak overnight:
  1 cup large lima beans
  3 cups fresh water

Bring to a boil in a pot:
  drained soaked beans
  4 cups fresh water
  3" strip of kombu (optional)

Or, if using canned beans:
  2½ cups cannellini or butter beans, drained and rinsed

Reduce heat to low, and simmer with the lid ajar for about 45 minutes, or until beans are soft. Drain beans and set aside.

Make the Lemon-Spinach Sauce, and pour it over the warm beans.

Serve warm or at room temperature.

Variation:
You can substitute small lima beans, navy beans or Great Northern beans for the large lima beans.

◆

LEMON-SPINACH SAUCE

A lush spring green sauce that especially complements white or lima beans, and also goes well with grains or vegetables.

In a blender, blend until smooth:

Preparation time: 5 minutes

Makes: ²/₃ cup

2–4 cloves garlic, peeled and minced
2 tablespoons fresh lemon juice
¼ cup olive oil
½ teaspoon salt
¼ teaspoon black pepper
2 cups fresh spinach leaves, chopped (without stems)

Serving idea: Serve Lima Beans with Lemon-Spinach Sauce with Carrot Salad or raw grated beets and a grain such as couscous.

◆

SEITAN

Seitan is wheat gluten, made of whole-wheat flour and water. It has a chewy, meat-like texture and can be boiled, baked, stir-fried, sliced for sandwiches or added to soups and stews. Wheat gluten is easy to digest, and has a high protein content, making it a healthy addition to a vegetarian diet. Though it can be found at natural food stores and some supermarkets, homemade seitan is less expensive and tastes a lot better. Look for wheat gluten flour at your local natural food store.

Mix in a bowl, to create a gluten dough:

Preparation time: 15 minutes

Cooking time: 30 minutes

Serves: 4

1 cup wheat gluten flour
¾ cup fresh water

Bring to a boil in a large pot:
2 cup fresh water
¼ cup tamari or Bragg
gluten dough
1½ inch fresh ginger root, sliced

Reduce heat to low and simmer, covered, for 10 minutes. Then, with a wooden spoon, turn dough upside down in the pot (during cooking the dough will expand, and might be sticking to the bottom, so loosen it first, then turn it). Cover and continue simmering for another 10 minutes.

Turn heat off and let cool for a few minutes. Then take gluten-dough out of the cooking water, and slice it into thin strips. Save any left over liquid from cooking. Discard ginger slices.

In a pan sauté for 5–10 minutes, on medium-high heat:
>2 tablespoons sunflower oil
>2 big cloves garlic, peeled and minced
>2 tablespoons ginger root, peeled and grated
>seitan slices

Cover pan while sautéing and stir frequently. You can add some of the left-over liquid to the pan for moisture, if it seems too dry.

When seitan pieces are crisp and golden, turn heat off and add:
>1 tablespoon fresh lemon juice
>1 teaspoon maple syrup

Serving idea:
Creates a lovely meal served over a plain grain and steamed vegetables with your favorite sauce.

◆

Vegetables

Steamed Vegetables

Stir-Fried Vegetables

Turnip-Rutabaga Sauté

Ginger Bok-Choy

Herbed Peas

Zucchini with Lime

Israeli Green Beans

Mushrooms with Thyme

Carrot Salad

STEAMED VEGETABLES

Almost any vegetable can be lightly and healthily cooked by steaming. You can also steam a variety of vegetables together.

Steaming requires a pot with a tight-fitting lid. You can use either a steamer pot (which is actually 2 pots, one of which has holes in the bottom and sits on top and slightly inside the other) or a collapsible metal steamer placed in a pot. It is always better to slightly under-steam vegetables so they don't get completely limp, and lose all their color and nutrients. Remember that even after you've turned the heat off, the steam will continue to cook the vegetables.

Some Vegetable Steaming Guidelines:

The denser the vegetable, the longer it takes to steam. Root and ground vegetables take between 5–30 minutes to steam, depending upon the vegetable, how old it is, and how large the pieces are (the smaller the pieces, the shorter the steaming time). Green leafy vegetables require only 3–10 minutes to steam, with tougher greens such as kale and collards taking longer than tender greens such as spinach or dandelion leaves.

Steaming Vegetables, Step-by-Step:

- Partially fill with fresh water—about 2 inches deep—the bottom of your steamer or a regular pot.
- Put the top part of the steamer, or the steamer basket, in the pot, cover it, and bring the water to a boil.
- Meanwhile, wash and chop or slice the vegetables.
- Once the water is boiling, place the vegetables in the steamer basket or top pot.
- Cover the pot, reduce the heat, and allow to steam until the vegetables are tender (when a fork can pierce them).

Cooking tips:

- When steaming different vegetables together, put the root or ground vegetables in the steamer first, and later add the leafy vegetables. For example, if you are mixing carrot, broccoli and collards, start steaming the carrot first, then add the broccoli, finishing by adding the collards. If you are steaming only leafy vegetables, start with the stems and add the leaves a little later.

- 3 cups of uncooked chopped greens yield 1 cup cooked greens.
- Save water from steaming greens and use it as vegetable broth for cooking grains or making soups.
- Check the water level after a few minutes to make sure that the water has not all boiled off.
- To flavor plain steamed vegetables, drizzle them with some olive oil, fresh lemon juice, or tamari before serving. See also the recipes for sauces and dressings.

◆

STIR-FRIED VEGETABLES

This recipe is just an example of the creative mix of vegetables that you can use to make a healthy, light lunch or dinner. Experiment with your own combinations to see what you enjoy most.

Sauté in a pan or a wok for about
8 minutes, until vegetables are crisp tender:

Preparation time: 10 minutes
Cooking time: 8 minutes
Serves: 3–4

    1–2 tablespoons sunflower oil
    1 carrot, peeled and cut into quarter rounds
    2 stalks celery, cut in half lengthwise, then diagonally into ½" pieces
    1 cup shredded green cabbage
    ½ cup red bell pepper, cut into small cubes
    1 zucchini, cut into half rounds
    1½ tablespoons sesame seeds

Keep tossing and stirring the vegetables. Then add and stir again to coat the vegetables:
    ½ teaspoon garlic powder
    1½ teaspoons tamari or Bragg

Turn heat off and sprinkle on top:
    ¼ cup fresh parsley leaves, minced

Serving idea:
Mix with plain cooked black-eyed peas or other cooked beans.

◆

TURNIP-RUTABAGA SAUTÉ

This simple sauté with salt brings out the natural sweetness of these hearty root vegetables.

Wash, peel and cut into quarter rounds:
    1 medium turnip
    1 medium rutabaga

Preparation time: 10 minutes
Cooking time: 20 minutes
Serves: 3–4

In a skillet, sauté:
    1 ½ tablespoons sesame oil
    rutabaga pieces (these take longer to cook than turnips)
    ½ teaspoon salt, sprinkled on top

After 5 minutes add:
    turnip pieces
    ½ teaspoon salt, sprinkled on top

Cover with a lid and cook on medium-low heat. Stir a few times, and when the vegetables start to caramelize (get brown), reduce the heat to low and continue to cook until they are soft (about 10 minutes in total). Usually the vegetables will sweat and release moisture, if not then add a little fresh water to prevent sticking and burning. Turn heat off and let sit covered for 5–10 minutes. If desired, drizzle a little tamari or Bragg over the cooked vegetables.

Serving idea:
A good match with plain quinoa and steamed mustard greens.

◆

GINGER BOK-CHOY

A light garnish of sesame and ginger adds an Oriental flavor to bok choy—a green vegetable from the cabbage family.

From a bunch of bok choy, separate and rinse well:

Preparation time: 5 minutes
Cooking time: 10–12 minutes
Makes: 1 cup
Serves: 1–2

    3 stems and leafy greens

(Save the rest of the bok choy in the refrigerator for another occasion.)

Slice the bok choy diagonally about ½" wide, and separate the white stems from the leafy portions.

Sauté in a pan for 5–8 minutes, covered:
    1 ½ tablespoons sesame oil
    1 tablespoon peeled and grated fresh ginger root
    bok choy stems (should be about 2 ½ cups)

Then toss in and simmer for 5 more minutes, covered:
    leafy greens (about 1 cup)

Turn heat off and drizzle over the top:
    1 tablespoon tamari or Bragg

Cover the pan again and let sit for 5 minutes to absorb flavors and finish cooking.

Serving idea:
Great with Sesame Brown Rice.

◆

Some Basic Recipes

HERBED PEAS

An Italian friend shared this unique treatment for frozen peas.

Sauté until golden, about 5–10 minutes:
   ¼ cup olive oil
   1 cup onion, minced
   2 cloves garlic, peeled and minced

Preparation time: 5 minutes
Cooking time: 10–15 minutes
Makes: 4 cup
Serves: 4–6

Mix in:
   2 teaspoons dried sage
   2 tablespoons nutritional yeast
   ⅓ cup fresh water (or tomato juice)
   4 cups frozen peas, thawed

Cover, reduce heat to low, and simmer for 10 minutes. Turn heat off and sprinkle with:
   ¼ cup fresh parsley leaves, minced

Serve warm.

Variation:
Steamed peas go also well with melted butter, salt, black pepper, and chopped fresh mint leaves.

Serving idea:
Goes well with French Lentil Paté, baked winter squash, green salad and tomato slices.

◆

ZUCCHINI WITH LIME

The refreshing scent and taste of lime add zest to this light summer vegetable.

Wash:
    4 zucchini

Preparation time: 10 minutes
Cooking time: 5–8 minutes
Serves: 3–4

Cut each zucchini into half lengthwise.
Then slice each half diagonally into ½" pieces.

Place in a bowl:
    zucchini pieces
    1 teaspoon salt

Let sit for 5 minutes. Then rinse zucchini and pat dry with a paper towel.

Saute for 5–8 minutes, until zucchini pieces are soft, but crisp:
    2 tablespoons olive oil or ghee
    4 cloves garlic, whole and peeled
    zucchini pieces

Discard garlic cloves and place zucchini in a bowl. Add:
    1 tablespoon fresh lime juice
    ½ teaspoon dried oregano
    2 tablespoons fresh parsley leaves, chopped
    salt and black pepper to taste

◆

Some Basic Recipes

ISRAELI GREEN BEANS

Slightly sweet, with a touch of tomato and herbs, tender green beans become a special treat.

Wash:
3/4 lb. (12 ounces) green beans

Snap the caps off, and steam the green beans until almost soft, about 8 minutes. Set aside.

Preparation time: 15 minutes
Cooking time: 20–25 minutes
Steaming time: 8 minutes
Serves: 4

Meanwhile, in a large pan, sauté for about 8 minutes until golden:
1 tablespoon sunflower oil
1/2 cup onion, minced
2 cloves garlic, peeled and minced

Add:
1 ripe medium tomato, cut into small cubes

Sauté until tomato cubes are very soft, about 10 minutes

Add steamed green beans and cook until they are tender, about 3–5 minutes.

Then add:
3/4 teaspoon dried oregano
3/4 teaspoon dried basil
1/2 teaspoon salt
1 1/2 teaspoons maple syrup

Mix all ingredients together, turn heat off and add salt to taste.

◆

95

MUSHROOMS WITH THYME

This easily prepared but elegant dish makes a tasty appetizer or side dish to a sumptuous meal.

In a skillet, sauté on medium heat, for
10 minutes:

Preparation time: 10 minutes
Cooking time: 10 minutes
Serves: 4

  ¼ cup ghee or olive oil
  2 big cloves garlic, peeled and minced
  1 teaspoon dried thyme
  ½ lb. button mushrooms, whole

Sauté until mushrooms are just soft and begin to release their juices. Stir frequently to be sure the mushrooms cook evenly. Turn heat off.

Place the mushrooms on a platter and drizzle over them:
  2 teaspoons fresh lemon juice
  pinch of salt and black pepper

Garnish with fresh parsley leaves.

◆

CARROT SALAD

A fresh, fat-free and quick salad for spring and summer.

Mix into a bowl:

Preparation time: 10 minutes
Cooking time: 10 minutes
Serves: 3–4

  1 tablespoon fresh lemon juice
  1 teaspoon fresh ginger root juice
    (for milder taste use only ½ teaspoon)
  1 teaspoon maple syrup
  2 tablespoons fresh cilantro leaves, minced

Add and mix well:
  2 cups carrots, peeled and grated

Let sit to absorb flavors, about 10 minutes. Serve.

◆

Soups

Miso Soup

Split Mung Soup

Daikon-Watercress Soup

Red Lentil and Root Vegetable Soup

Green Split Pea Soup

MISO SOUP

Miso, a fermented soy paste, makes a hearty broth that you can use as the base for many vegetable soup combinations. Try different kinds of miso to see what you prefer.

Bring to a boil:
    1 cup fresh water or vegetable broth

Preparation time: 2–3 minutes
Serves: 1

In a soup bowl place:
    1½ teaspoons mellow miso paste (or any kind you like)

When the water boils, remove it from the heat. Pour ⅓ cup of water into the bowl with the miso paste, and stir to dissolve the paste. Then add the rest of the boiling water.

Variations: (What to add to the miso broth)
- Chopped kombu from cooking beans, or a toasted nori sheet, cut into thin strips.
- Wakame and tofu:

   Before making the miso broth, soak a few strips of wakame seaweed in fresh water until soft, about 5 minutes. Drain the water off and squeeze the wakame to get rid of excess water. Cut away any hard ribs and chop it coarsely.

   Cut 3 oz. of firm tofu, into ½" cubes. Steam or boil tofu cubes for about 5 minutes. Add wakame and tofu to miso broth.
- Tofu, spinach leaves and shiitake mushroom:

   Before making the miso broth, soak one dried shiitake mushroom in hot water to cover it, until soft, about 20 minutes. Slice the mushroom.

   Prepare tofu as above, and wash 1 or 2 leaves of spinach.

   Add shiitake slices, tofu, and spinach leaves to miso broth.
- Add minced green onions, grated carrot or daikon, tofu, mushroom, wakame, or spinach in any combination.

◆

SPLIT MUNG SOUP

The golden color of split mung beans, which are a staple food of India, adds to the soothing quality of this nutritious soup. Mung beans are very easy to digest, and a good source of protein.

In a pot sauté for 5 minutes:

    Preparation time: 10 minutes
    Cooking time: 30 minutes
    Serves: 4–5

    1 cup onion, minced
    1 cup green cabbage, minced
    1 cup carrot, peeled and chopped
    1 cup zucchini, chopped
    1 cup turnip, peeled and chopped (optional)

Add:

    1 cup split mung beans, rinsed
    6 cups fresh water

Bring to a boil, reduce heat to low and simmer, with the lid ajar, for about 30 minutes.

Let cool 5–10 minutes, then blend in a food processor.

While blending add:

    $\frac{1}{3}$ cup fresh parsley leaves, chopped
    1 tablespoon salt or to taste

Serve warm.

Variations:

1. Add to sautéed vegetables:

    $\frac{1}{2}$ teaspoon garlic powder
    1 tablespoon fresh ginger root, peeled and grated
    1 teaspoon dried thyme

or:

    $\frac{1}{2}$ teaspoon cumin powder
    $\frac{1}{2}$ teaspoon ground coriander

2. You can use any kind of beans such as: red lentils, garbanzos, black-eyed peas, or white beans. Adjust the soaking and cooking times according to kind of bean you use.

Serving idea:
Serve with baked or boiled beets.

DAIKON-WATERCRESS SOUP

Daikon is an Oriental white radish that is actually quite mild when cooked. Paired with watercress, it makes a healthy, soothing soup, especially after a stressful day.

In a pot sauté for 3 minutes:
    2 tablespoons sesame oil
    2 cups, daikon, peeled and cut into quarter rounds

Preparation time: 5 minutes
Cooking time: 15 minutes
Serves: 4

Add:
    4 cups fresh water

Bring to a boil and add:
    5 cups watercress, chopped (stems and leaves)

Reduce heat to low and simmer, covered for10 minutes. Turn heat off and add:
    ¼ cup tamari or Bragg
    1½ teaspoons Spike or to taste

◆

RED LENTIL AND ROOT VEGETABLE SOUP

Sautéed root vegetables lend their sweetness to this golden-colored soup.

In a pot sauté for about 5 minutes:
- 2 tablespoons sunflower oil
- 1 medium onion, chopped
- 2 stalks celery, coarsely chopped
- 1 medium carrot, peeled and chopped
- 1 medium rutabaga, peeled and chopped

Preparation time: 10 minutes
Cooking time: 40 minutes
Serves: 4

Add:
- 1 cup red lentils, rinsed
- 2 bay leaves
- 1 1/2 teaspoons dried oregano
- 4 cups fresh water

Bring to a boil, reduce heat to low, and simmer with the lid ajar, for about 30–40 minutes, until lentils and vegetables are soft. Turn heat off. Let cool for 5–10 minutes. Discard bay leaves.

Blend in batches in a food processor, and add:
- 1 teaspoon salt or to taste

◆

GREEN SPLIT PEA SOUP

Silky green with a hint of ginger, this soup makes a colorful entree in a festive meal.

Soak overnight:
    1 cup green split peas, rinsed
    3 cups fresh water

Preparation time: 10 minutes
Soaking time: Overnight
Cooking time: 45 minutes
Serves: 4

Bring to a boil in a large pot:
    drained, soaked peas
    ½ medium onion, minced (about ⅔ cup)
    ¼ cup fresh ginger root, peeled and grated
    4½ cups fresh water

Reduce heat to low and simmer, with the lid ajar, for about 40 minutes, until peas are soft. Turn heat off, and let sit for 5–10 minutes to cool.

Blend in blender in small batches or in food processor. (A blender will create a smoother, silkier texture.)

Add while blending:
    2 tablespoons olive oil
    2 teaspoons salt or to taste.

Garnish with fresh parsley sprigs.

◆

DRESSINGS AND SAUCES

Here are a variety of dressings and sauces that are easy to prepare and add taste and flavor to plain grains, beans and steamed vegetables. You can make them ahead of time and keep them in the refrigerator for 3–6 days.

SAUCES

Garlic-Parsley Sauce

Peanut Sauce

Orange-Ginger Sauce

Italian Tomato Sauce

SALAD DRESSINGS

Ginger Dressing

Tahini-Dill Dressing

Dijon-Cilantro Salad Dressing

Miso Dressing

GARLIC–PARSLEY SAUCE

If you like garlic, this sauce is for you. It adds lively taste and color to cooked grains or steamed vegetables.

Blend in a blender until smooth:
   ½ cup olive oil
   2 big cloves garlic, peeled and minced,
      (about 2 teaspoons, minced)
   ¼ cup fresh parsley leaves, minced
   ½ teaspoon salt

Preparation time: 5 minutes
Makes: ¾ cup

◆

PEANUT SAUCE

A spicy sauce in the Thai tradition, this is delicious on plain grains, mixed grains, and raw or steamed vegetables.

Blend in a blender, until smooth:
   2 tablespoons sesame oil
   1 tablespoon fresh ginger root juice (see page 106)
   ⅛ teaspoon dried red chili pepper
   ⅓ cup packed fresh cilantro leaves
   2 tablespoons peanut butter
   ¼ cup fresh water
   2 teaspoons tamari or Bragg
   1 teaspoon honey

Preparation time: 10 minutes
Makes: ⅔ cup

◆

ORANGE-GINGER SAUCE

Completely fat-free, this spicy-sweet sauce nicely complements grated raw beets or jicama, and steamed vegetables.

Mix in a bowl: **Preparation time:** 5 minutes
    ¼ cup fresh orange juice   **Makes:** ½ cup
    2 tablespoons fresh lemon juice
    1 tablespoon maple syrup
    1½ teaspoons fresh ginger root juice (see page 106)

Serving idea:
Try this sauce on a salad of grated beets and toasted walnuts, with a garnish of fresh cilantro.

◆

ITALIAN TOMATO SAUCE

You will love this sweet fresh tomato sauce which uses only natural ingredients—no canned tomatoes or refined sugar. Serve it on grains or vegetables, or as a pasta sauce.

Preparation time: 15 minutes
In a small sauce pan sauté for about 5 minutes: **Cooking time:** 25 minutes
    1 tablespoon sunflower oil   **Makes:** 1¼ cups
    ½ red onion, minced (about ½ cup)   **Serves:** 2–3
    1 large clove garlic, peeled and minced

Add and mix:
    2 medium-size, ripe tomatoes, cut into small cubes

Simmer for 10 minutes. Turn heat off, and blend in a blender until smooth.

Return to pot and add:
    ¼ cup fresh water
    ⅓ cup raw butternut squash, peeled and grated
    2 tablespoons olive oil
    ½ teaspoon dried basil
    1 teaspoon nutritional yeast
    ¼ teaspoon salt

Cover and simmer for 10 minutes. Turn heat off and serve warm.

GINGER DRESSING

Use this tangy dressing to flavor steamed vegetables. It's especially good with broccoli.

In a bowl mix together until blended:
    1/2 cup ghee, melted
    2 tablespoons fresh ginger root juice
        (use 1 tablespoon for milder flavor)
    1 tablespoon plus 1 teaspoon fresh lemon juice
    1 tablespoon plus 1 teaspoon tamari or Bragg

Preparation time: 5 minutes
Makes: 3/4 cup

Cooking tips:
To make fresh ginger root juice: Grate whole, fresh ginger root. Place a small amount at a time into your palm, and squeeze its juice into a bowl. Discard ginger pulp.

This amount of dressing will be enough for 4 heads of broccoli. (Each head of broccoli may serve up to 4.)

Store the dressing in the refrigerator. Take it out of the refrigerator when you begin your meal preparations, or at least 15 minutes before use, to allow it to come to room temperature so it will be pourable.

Variation:
Instead of ghee, use olive oil or 1/4 cup oil and 1/4 cup vegetable broth.

◆

TAHINI-DILL DRESSING

A light summery dressing that is sweet and refreshing on green salad. It also makes a lovely sauce for plain Basmati white rice, steamed kale and carrot, and plain garbanzo beans.

Blend in a blender until smooth:

Preparation time: 10 minutes
Makes: 1¾ cup

- ¾ cup fresh water (2–3 tablespoons less for thicker consistency)
- ¼ cup olive oil
- ¼ cup fresh lemon juice
- ½ cup tahini (organic, roasted)
- 1 tablespoon maple syrup
- 2 teaspoons tamari or Bragg
- ½ teaspoon garlic powder
- ½ teaspoon dill weed
- ¼ teaspoon salt
- 1 pinch black pepper

◆

DIJON-CILANTRO SALAD DRESSING

This dressing is great over fresh green salad and steamed vegetables such as broccoli, cauliflower, and green beans.

Place in a blender:

Preparation time: 15 minutes
Makes: 1¼ cups

    ¼ cup fresh lemon juice
    1½ tablespoons Dijon mustard
    2 tablespoons tamari or Bragg
    1 teaspoon maple syrup or honey
    ¼ cup fresh cilantro leaves, packed
    ¼ cup fresh water

Blend on medium-high speed for a few seconds, then lower the speed and slowly add:

    2 tablespoons sesame oil
    ⅓ cup olive oil

Blend until smooth.

◆

MISO DRESSING

A zesty golden-hued sauce for grains, beans, steamed vegetables, or fresh green salad. It is especially good on plain quinoa, black-eyed peas, and steamed kale.

Blend in a blender until smooth:
 ½ cup sunflower oil
 1 tablespoon sesame oil
 2 tablespoons fresh lemon juice
 ¼ cup fresh water
 2 tablespoons mellow miso
 1 tablespoon fresh ginger root, peeled and grated, or 1 teaspoon
  fresh ginger root juice

Preparation time: 5 minutes
Makes: 1 cup

Variation: For an oil-free dressing—

Blend in a blender until smooth:
 1½ tablespoons mellow miso
 1 tablespoon fresh lemon juice
 1 tablespoon fresh ginger root, peeled and grated
 ¼ cup fresh water

Preparation time: 5 minutes
Makes: About ½ cup

◆

CHAPTER EIGHT

How to Plan a Menu

There are many reasons to plan menus in advance. Besides saving time and money on grocery shopping, it's also a good way to ensure that you are eating a well-balanced diet.

Most people who plan their meals in advance do it weekly. But one friend of mine plans a month ahead. She has found that planning menus helps her to stay within her budget, saves time, and ensures that her family has plenty of variety in their meals. Since she knows each day what she must do for each meal, she can do some of the preparation ahead of time.

General Daily Menu

One of the keys to a balanced diet is eating regular meals. If you plan healthy meals, and eat each meal at about the same time each day, you'll be less likely to snack on junk foods. Your energy levels will remain steady throughout the day, and your digestion will be stronger.

BREAKFAST—Breakfast should be a nutritious, simple to prepare meal. Nutrition research has shown that eating a good breakfast supports learning and is important especially for those who are trying to lose weight. Try to vary your breakfast foods from day to day.

LUNCH—Since digestion for most people is strongest in the middle of the day, it is best to eat your largest meal around noontime. A good lunch will keep your energy steady throughout the day and should include:

A cooked grain, a legume dish, a steamed or sautéed vegetable dish, and a raw green salad with grated or chopped raw vegetables such as tomato, cucumber, carrot, beet, jicama, sprouts, or olives. Nuts or seeds can be used as a garnish, and a sauce and salad dressing completes the meal.

DINNER—Eat a lighter meal at dinner, so that the digestive system is not overburdened when it is time to go to sleep. It could include:

Vegetable or bean soup, bread or a grain dish, and a raw salad.

SNACKS, DESSERT AND BEVERAGES

Fruit is best eaten alone, between meals as a snack. This is because they are digested more quickly and can ferment in the system if consumed on top of a more complex food.

Dessert could be eaten 3–4 times a week, always in moderation. If you are eating regular, balanced meals, you'll find that your craving for sweets will lessen, and you'll feel satisfied with an occasional treat.

It is important to drink plenty of water (8 cups a day, at room temperature), but not immediately before or after a meal (it dilutes the digestive juices). Herbal tea is a good alternative to coffee, black tea, and sodas.

In general, daily consumption of two servings each of grains, legumes and vegetables with the addition of a small amount of nuts, seeds and fruit is a good start. There is no fixed amount of each of the food groups that one should consume. Some people will need more protein in their diet (more beans and tofu), while others may need more grains. With time and experience you will know how much grain, beans, vegetables, nuts, seeds and fruits your body needs, and which ones are best for you.

If you have special medical circumstances, you should consult a nutritionist or a certified health practitioner before making any radical changes in your diet.

SIGNS OF IMBALANCE

- If you are eliminating meat entirely, but still consuming large amounts of cheese and chocolate you are probably getting too much saturated fat.
- In a vegetarian diet, there can be a tendency to go for too many carbohydrates and sugar, too little protein and vegetables. Eating lots of beans and grains and only small amounts of vegetables, greens and fruits can cause you to feel sluggish and heavy. Too much bread, potatoes, pasta, eggs, canned and frozen vegetables, sugar and coffee is unbalanced and fattening.
- Raw foods are good for cleansing, but consuming only fruit and raw vegetables can cause you to feel ungrounded, lightheaded and dizzy.

Menu Guidelines and Principles of Diet and Proper Eating

- Keep individual dishes simple. A combination of too many ingredients can be difficult for the digestive system to process.
- Use simple methods of cooking, treating the foods in ways that maintain their freshness.
- Make meals that are easy to digest, leaving you light and energetic. If they are tasty and nutritious, you will feel satisfied.
- Use ingredients and cooking styles according to the season. Shop in your local farmers' market for fresh seasonal items.

In summer and spring use more raw vegetables and fruits, and make cold salads, spreads, dips, and light grains. Steam, stir-fry, sauté, marinate, and grill foods.

In the fall and winter cook hearty soups, stews, casseroles, hardier grains and root vegetables. Dry roast grains, nuts and seeds and boil, bake, steam, or sauté foods.

- Add a variety of textures to your daily meals—crunchy, chewy and smooth.
- Combine the various vegetable groups (root, ground, leafy), use medleys of grains and beans, and vary your cooking techniques.
- Use fresh and dried herbs for subtle spicing. Avoid mixing too many flavors and different tastes in one dish.
- Create colorful meals. Include foods that are green, red orange, yellow, white and brown. This will help to keep your diet balanced.

- Eat three meals a day, at regular intervals; or up to 5 small meals a day. Make lunch your main meal, and have a lighter meal in the evening. If you can't do this, then at least wait three hours after dinner before you go to bed.
- Don't overeat. When you finish a meal you should feel comfortable, and as if you still have room in your stomach.
- Avoid drinking with meals, as this dilutes gastric juices and makes digestion less effective. This is especially true of iced drinks. Take fluids ½ hour before or 2 hours after meals. Drinking with meals also causes a tendency to obesity
- It is best to have desserts 2–3 hours after meals. The bigger the meal the fewer the enzymes there are available to digest desserts.
- As much as possible, avoid foods that have undergone extensive technological processing—irradiation, canning, freezing, etc.
- When eating out, try to avoid fast foods, meat, heavy fried foods, and sweets.
- Use easy, simpler recipes during the week and save the more labor intensive recipes for weekends, or when you have more time.
- Find creative ways to incorporate leftovers into the next meal.

CHAPTER NINE

Suggested Menus

The menus below were formed around the recipes in this book. Each menu combines a grain, legume, and vegetables whose colors, textures, and tastes complement one another. Some menus include some simple dishes, such as a steamed vegetable, that is not included in this book as a recipe. In the list below, the titles of recipes in this book are capitalized.

For a balanced, healthy diet, it's good to have both cooked and raw foods. Include your favorite raw salads with the menus below.

SPRING AND SUMMER BREAKFASTS

(If you have a good organic source, and can eat dairy and eggs, then add yogurt or cottage cheese, or other dairy products, and eggs occasionally.)

- Whole grain cereals, on a rotating basis: Granola, Muesli, plain buckwheat, plain millet, plain Jasmine rice, plain quinoa, oatmeal
- Whole wheat bread with nut butters

- Assorted fresh fruits, or fruit smoothies
- For garnishes on cereals, or incorporated in smoothies: nuts, seeds, unsulfured dried fruits, ghee, honey, maple syrup, oat bran, wheat germ
- Beverages such as: fruit juices, rice, soy or nut milk, herbal teas.

AUTUMN AND WINTER BREAKFASTS

(If you have a good organic source, and can eat dairy and eggs, then add yogurt or cottage cheese, or other dairy products, and eggs occasionally.)

- Hearty whole grain cereals on a rotating basis: Oat Groats, Steel Cut Oats, plain barley, Rice-Cocount Cereal, plain brown rice
- Whole wheat bread with nut butter
- Cooked or stewed fruits
- For garnishes on cereals: nuts, seeds, unsulfured dried fruits, ghee, honey, maple syrup, oat bran, wheat germ
- Beverages such as: fruit juices, rice, soy or nut milk, herbal teas.

SPRING AND SUMMER LUNCHES

French Lentil Paté

Pita bread

Stir-Fried Vegetables

•

Plain couscous

Plain garbanzo beans

Zucchini with Lime

Tahini-Dill Dressing

•

Black Eyed Pea Salad

Plain bulgur

Garlic-Parsley Sauce

•

Hummus

Zucchini with Lime

Pita bread

•

Lima Beans with Lemon-
   Spinach Sauce
Plain Jasmine rice
Steamed peas and carrots

•

Baked Marinated Tofu (sweet)
Plain millet
Mixed steamed greens (collards,
   beet greens, chard)
Lemon-Spinach Sauce

•

Tempeh Croutons
Wild Rice Salad
Mushrooms with Thyme
Italian Tomato Sauce

•

Plain black beans
Peanut Sauce
Whole wheat tortillas
Raw vegetables

•

Golden Millet
Herbed Peas
Carrot Salad
Baked Marinated Tofu

•

Mediterranean Navy Bean
   Spread
Plain bulgur
Garlic-Parsley Sauce
Steamed kale, collard greens,
   and dandelion greens

•

Stir-Fried Vegetables
Plain black-eyed peas

•

Summer Kamut Salad
Corn on the cob

•

Plain white Basmati rice
Steamed kale and carrots
Plain garbanzo beans
Tahini-Dill Dressing
Garlic-Parsley Sauce

•

Plain quinoa
Plain black-eyed peas
Stir-Fried Vegetables
Miso Dressing

•

SPRING AND SUMMER DINNERS

Serve soups with whole wheat bread, crackers, tortillas, or plain grains,
with a bean spread.

Miso Soup
Multi-grain bread
  •

Mediterranean Navy Bean
   Spread
Steamed broccoli, cauliflower
   and carrots
Pita bread
  •

Udon or buckwheat noodles
Italian Tomato Sauce
Steamed zucchini and red bell
   pepper
  •

Carrot Salad
Baked Marinated Tofu
Corn on the cob
  •

Plain quinoa
Stir-Fried Vegetables
Garlic-Parsley Sauce
  •

Pinto Beans Mexicana
Tortillas
Steamed or raw mixed
   vegetables
  •

Steamed cauliflower, carrot,
   and spinach
Ginger-Orange Sauce
Plain garbanzo beans
Plain couscous
  •

Plain bulgur
Steamed collard greens
Tahini-Dill Dressing
  •

AUTUMN AND WINTER LUNCHES

Seitan
Plain brown rice
Tahini-Dill Dressing
Steamed broccoli and carrot

•

Baked Marinated Tofu (salty)
Ginger Bok-Choy
Sesame Brown Rice

•

Crispy Herbed Tofu
Herbed Rice and Amaranth
Steamed Napa cabbage and
    mustard greens
Orange-Ginger Sauce

•

Lima Beans with Lemon-
    Spinach Sauce
Quinoa-Carrot Pilaf

•

Soybean-Spinach Curry
Plain Jasmine rice
Steamed carrots

•

Sesame Tempeh
Herbed Rice and Amaranth
Steamed spinach
Italian Tomato Sauce

•

Plain aduki beans
Sesame Brown Rice
Ginger Bok-Choy

•

Plain black beans
Golden Millet
Steamed mustard and turnip
    greens
Garlic-Parsley Dressing

•

Pinto Beans Mexicana
Plain quinoa
Baked winter squash

•

Tofu, Rice and Vegetables in
    the Rice-Cooker
Peanut Sauce

•

Buckwheat and Quinoa Salad
Steamed carrot, cauliflower
   and broccoli
Orange-Ginger Sauce
   •

Barley-Wheat Berry-Millet
   Medley
Steamed turnip, pea and
   carrot
Tahini-Dill Dressing
   •

Israeli Green Beans
Plain quinoa
Crispy Herbed Tofu
Italian Tomato Sauce
   •

French Lentil Paté
Quinoa-Carrot Pilaf
Steamed green beans
Tahini-Dill Dressing
   •

Plain Basmati rice
Plain garbanzo beans
Steamed spinach and chard
Tahini-Dill Dressing
   •

Steamed green beans
Garlic-Parsley Sauce
Baked banana squash
Green Split Pea Soup
Tortillas or rice crackers
   •

AUTUMN AND WINTER DINNERS

Quinoa-Carrot Pilaf
Steamed broccoli
Ginger Dressing
   •

Buckwheat and Quinoa Salad
Ginger Bok-Choy
   •

Green Split Pea Soup
Baked Squash
   •

Noodles
Turnip-Rutabaga Sauté
Tahini-Dill Dressing
   •

Plain aduki beans
Steamed kale, bok choy, and
    collard greens
Miso Dressing

•

Plain Brown Rice
Steamed carrot, napa cabbage,
    bok-choy, collards, ginger
Miso Dressing

•

Daikon-Watercress Soup
Golden Millet

•

Red Lentils and Root Vegetable
    Soup
Whole wheat bread

•

Green Split Pea Soup
Herbed Rice and Amaranth

•

Baked butternut squash
Plain quinoa
Lemon-Spinach Sauce

•

Green Split Pea Soup
Quinoa-Carrot Pilaf
Steamed collard greens
Peanut Sauce

•

Baked banana squash
Lentil Paté
Herbed Peas
Pita Bread

•

Baked Marinated Tofu
Plain quinoa
Mixed collards, beet greens,
    chard
Ginger Dressing

•

About the Author

Blanche Agassy McCord was the head chef at The Expanding Light Yoga and Meditation Retreat for seven years, where she now teaches yoga, meditation, and vegetarian cooking classes. She learned Kosher and vegetarian cooking while growing up in Israel, studied Japanese cooking while living in Kyoto, Japan, and learned Ayurvedic, macrobiotic, and Indian cooking from premier California chefs.

Bibliography

Agassy McCord, Blanche, *Global Kitchen*, Crystal Clarity, 1997.

Walters, J. Donald, *The Art and Science of Raja Yoga*, Crystal Clarity, 2000.

Ornish, Dean, *Everyday Cooking with Dr. Dean Ornish*, Harper Collins, 1996.

Morningstar, Amadea, *Ayurvedic Cooking for Westerners*, Lotus Press, 1995.

Robbins, John, *May All Be Fed*, William Morrow and Company, Inc., 1992.

Wood, Rebecca, *The New Whole Foods Encyclopedia*, Penguin Putnam Inc., 1999.

Colbin, Annemarie, *Food And Healing*, Ballantine Books, 1986.

Sheldon, Margen, *The Wellness Encyclopedia Of Food and Nutrition*, Rebus, 1992.

Robertson, Robin and Jon, *The Sacred Kitchen*, New World Library, 1999.

Sri Yukteswar, Swami, *The Holy Science*, Self Realization Fellowship, 1990.

Saltzman, Joanne, *Amazing Grains*, Schuettge and Carleton, 1990.

Martin, Jeanne Marie, *The All Natural Allergy Cookbook*, Harbour Publishing, 1992.

Banchek, Linda, *Cooking For Life*, Harmony Books, 1989.

Ferre', Julia, **Basic Macrobiotic Cooking,** George Ohsawa Macrobiotic Foundation, 1987.

Robertson, Laurel, Carol Flinders, and Brian Ruppenthal, **The New Laurel's Kitchen,** Ten Speed Press, 1986.

Lad, Usha and Dr. Vasant, **Ayurvedic Cooking for Self-Healing,** The Ayurvedic Press, 1994.

Gates, Donna, **The Body Ecology Diet,** B.E.D. Publications, 1993.

Pickarski, Brother Ron, **Friendly Foods,** Ten Speed Press, 1991.

Index

About the *for Starters* series

The "... *for Starters*" series was created to give both beginning and long-time practitioners a brief yet thorough introduction to some of the most popular spiritual topics and practices of our day. More than mere overviews, the books in this series will help you quickly gain a foothold of understanding—and even more importantly—they will help you find the enthusiasm and energy necessary to incorporate these principles and practices into your daily life. That is, they actively help you get *started*.

Titles in the "for Starters" series

Meditation for Starters
J. Donald Walters

Meditation brings balance into our lives, providing an oasis of profound rest and renewal. Doctors are prescribing it for a variety of stress-related diseases. This award-winning book offers simple but powerful guidelines for attaining inner peace. Learn to prepare the body and mind for meditation, special breathing techniques, ways to focus and "let go," develop superconscious awareness, sharp-en your willpower, and increase intuition and calmness. Taught by J. Donald Walters, an internationally respected spiritual teacher who has practiced meditation daily for over fifty years. *Meditation for Starters* is available as a book & CD set, book & cassette set, and as a video. Each item is also sold separately.

Yoga for Starters
Gyandev McCord

A unique and innovative introduction to this popular topic, *Yoga for Starters* is a handy lay-flat reference book that covers the basic principles of yoga. Includes sections on standing poses, relaxation poses, spinal stretches, inverted and sitting poses, all with photographs. Also includes suggestions for routines of varying lengths from beginning to advanced study. Most importantly, *Yoga for Starters* gives a broad overview of what yoga is and the main principles and practices associated with it. In addition to a section on yoga postures, there are also chapters on yoga philosophy, breathing, healing principles, and meditation.

Intuition for Starters
J. Donald Walters

Every day we are confronted with difficult problems and thorny situations for which we either don't have enough information to make clear-cut decisions or for which there is no easy intellectual answer. At these moments, we all wish that there was another way to know how to make the right choice. Fortunately, there is another way: through using our intuition. More than just a "feeling" or a guess, true intuition is one of the most important—yet often least developed—of our human faculties. Often thought of as something vague and undefinable, many people mistakenly assume that intuition cannot be understood and developed. *Intuition for Starters* will explain what true intuition is, where it comes from, the practices and attitudes necessary for developing it, and how to tap into intuitive guidance at will.

Chakras for Starters
Savitri Simpson

Long a popular subject in metaphysical and Eastern spirituality circles, interest in the chakras has recently spread into the mainstream. Yet, for all of the newfound interest, until now, there has yet to be written a concise, easy-to-read guide to this most intriguing of all topics. In *Chakras for Starters*, Savitri Simpson demystifies and explains what chakras are, how to work with them, and the benefits accrued from doing so. Readers will learn how working with the chakras can help them feel a greater sense of security, self-control, heartfulness, centeredness, intuition, and spiritual transformation.

Also Available from Crystal Clarity

Global Kitchen
Vegetarian Favorites from The Expanding Light Yoga Retreat
Blanche Agassy McCord

The Expanding Light retreat center, well-known worldwide, has served these simple, wonderful recipes for many years. This is the first cookbook from an established yoga retreat where, according to a recent Arthur Frommer's syndicated travel column, the guests gave the only "high rating" for the meals. Conscious cooking, treating the food with respect, love, and focused attention are some of the secrets of success.

Simply Vegetarian!
Easy-to-Prepare Recipes for the Vegetarian Gourmet
Nancy Mair

Gourmet, easy-to-prepare dishes that are actually tasty and nutritious! Reflecting many of the most current trends in gourmet cooking, *Simply Vegetarian!* is ideal both for those who are transitioning into vegetarian eating and long-time vegetarians eager to discover some wonderful new recipes. This winning combination includes 50 main dishes as well as a complete selection of soups, salads, and stunning deserts that make for a complete meal. Easy to follow directions, easy to find ingredients, and meals that can be prepared in 30 minutes or less. *Simply Vegetarian!* is widely regarded as one of the classics!

MUSIC FOR COOKING FROM CLARITY SOUND & LIGHT

Relax
Meditations for Piano
David Miller

Let peace gently enfold you as you listen to these lilting melodies. This soothing instrumental music is the perfect antidote to stress of all types. Calming and inspiring, it will lift you above day-to-day worries and cares. Play it after work, before falling asleep or anytime you want to banish tensions and troubles . . . .

Secrets of Love
Melodies to Open Your Heart
Donald Walters

Unlike any music you have ever heard, Secrets of Love will transform your life. Each musical selection captures the essence of one of the many aspects of love. Perfect as background music, "mood" music, or music for relaxation, all eighteen songs can also be actively used as dynamic tools for awakening the loving qualities within your heart.

Mystic Harp 2
Derek Bell

Derek Bell is the legendary harpist of The Chieftains. Original melodies by Donald Walters capture the mystical quality of traditional Celtic music. Derek plays Celtic harp on each of the twenty richly orchestrated melodies. A beautiful sequel to the first Bell/Walters best-selling collaboration, *The Mystic Harp*.

Himalayan Sunrise
Sitar and Tabla Backgrounds for Vitality
Agni with Lewis Howard

This new album features flowing, gently energizing music which, like the sun rising over the mountains, softly awakens listeners, recharges their minds and bodies, and helps them remain calmly energetic throughout the day.

For a free Crystal Clarity catalog, or to place an order, please call 800-424-1055 or 530-478-7600 Or visit our website: www.crystalclarity.com